FURTHER FASTER
THE ULTIMATE GUIDE TO ACCELERATING YOUR CAREER

WARREN JAMES

First published in Australia 2020 by Rapid Mentoring
Copyright © 2020 Warren James
rapidmentoring.com.au

All rights reserved. No part of this publication may be reproduced, stored in or entered into a retrieval system, or transmitted, in any form, or by any means (electronic, mechanical, photocopying, recording or otherwise) without the prior written permission of the publisher.

The rights of Warren James to be identified as the author of this work has been asserted by him in accordance with the *Copyright, Designs and Patents Act 1988.*

This book is sold subject to the condition that it shall not, by way of trade or otherwise, be lent, resold, hired out, or otherwise circulated without the publisher's prior consent in any form of binding or cover other than that in which it's published and without a similar condition including this condition being imposed on the subsequent purchaser.

Author: Warren James
Title: *Further Faster – The Ultimate Guide to Accelerating Your Career*
ISBN: 9780648910602

Subjects: Career Development, Professional Development
Book Production Services: Bev Ryan, www.bevryanpublish.com
Illustrations: Warren James

This book is not intended to provide personalised legal, financial, or investment advice. The author and the publisher specifically disclaim any liability, loss or risk incurred as a consequence, directly or indirectly, of the use and application of any contents of this work.

A catalogue record for this book is available from the National Library of Australia

WHAT OTHERS ARE SAYING

The Rapid Online Mentoring program—all the advice, tips and tricks for entering and landing in the career path/life direction you really want. From new starter to manager, it offers career progression and advice on setting yourself up for a life of independence and freedom. Take the shortcuts in life by using someone else's experience—life hacks 101.

—Lee Thompson, Rapid FastTrack member

Rapid Online Mentoring is a holistic program that combines clear insight and valuable self-reflective activities in such a way that not only are you taking your career to the next level, you're also finding out more about yourself and your purpose. I wish this program had been around when I first started in the corporate world.

—Jade Hannam, Rapid FastTrack member

Who inspires you? Who makes up your tribe of believers that keep pushing you forward at all costs? Warren James, founder of Rapid Online Mentoring, is an inspiration to me. Although only in his mid-thirties, he's already created an impactful business, and is a pillar of empowerment for an entire community of young professionals, myself included. Mentoring is an interesting area that is ripe for disruption, and Warren has cracked the mentoring code. If you're a young professional in need of support from like-minded superstars, check out what's available through Rapid Online Mentoring. You will not regret the five minutes spent on looking it up.

—Janenie Mohgan, Rapid FastTrack member

CONTENTS

Preface 7
Acknowledgements 13
Introduction 15

PART 1 PLAN YOUR JOURNEY 21
   1 Find Direction in Life 23
      Personality tests 25
      Values 27
      What you are capable of 30
      You are enough 32
   2 Four Pillars 37
      Personal life 40
      Career goals 44
      Bucket list 51
      Finances 54
   3 Sticky-Note Planner 65
   4 Discovering Your Purpose 71
   5 Phased Attention 75

PART 2 PACK YOUR BAGS 79
   6 Preparation 81
      Motivation 82
      Fears 85
   7 Confidence 93
   8 Strengths 95
   9 Mental Strength 99

   Recharge your batteries *102*
   Gratitude *103*
 10 Stress. 105
   Switching off *109*
   Sleep *111*
 11 Learning to Prioritise 119
 12 Adapting to Change. 121
   Kübler-Ross model *122*
   Corporate change *124*

PART 3 ACCELERATE YOUR JOURNEY. **129**
 13 The Execution. 131
   Tips from the pros *132*
 14 Routines and Habits 135
 15 Flow States. 137
 16 Multitasking. 145
 17 Procrastination 149
 18 Asking the Right Questions. 153
 19 Learning to Read Faster 157
 20 Career Progression 161
   Career-Limiting Moves. *163*
 21 From Technician to Manager to Leader. 165
 22 Becoming a Prominent Person in Your Industry 169
 23 Negotiating Like a Pro 173
   Salary negotiation *178*
 24 Performance Reviews. 181

Conclusion. **189**
Make More Out of Your Life and Career in Less Time **191**
The Script **194**
References, Resources And Further Reading. **197**

PREFACE

I grew up in Victoria, Australia, on a 250-hectare beef-cattle farm. Life was pretty good. There was plenty of space, and a motorbike to throw a leg over for a ride in the sprawling paddocks.

There was always a parental push towards academia, as Dad didn't see a future in farming and always dreamed of me fulfilling his own personal dream of going to university. He would always give me the unfavourable jobs on the farm to deter me from wanting to take up a life on the land. I spent hours driving the open-cab tractor up and down the paddock in 42-degree summer heat, or chipping weeds with a shovel, herding cattle, or even bouncing around on earthmoving equipment.

School came pretty easily to me, and I never needed to apply much effort to maintain reasonably high grades. I rarely did homework, and I never tried all that hard to get a good university entry score because I was fearful of getting into a difficult degree. Physics, maths and graphic design were always my stronger points. English, on the other hand, was a constant struggle. Ironically, here I am, writing a book.

Following year twelve I studied electronic engineering in Melbourne. I had no idea what I actually wanted to study, but I liked the campus and the course sounded kind of interesting. After partying too much in first year I ended up failing a few subjects, which meant my four-year degree became a five-year degree.

My parents paid for my rent for the first two years, but I had to come up with my own spending money. This was great for learning how to manage money and a budget. I got a job in the university bar, setting up speakers for bar night. It paid $50 per week, plus free beer on the night.

Towards the end of my second year at university I came down with glandular fever. After I recovered, I had no desire to go out drinking. This meant my evenings were free to actually study and keep up with my subjects. Consequently my grades went from barely passing to all B's and A's.

After five long years of effectively putting myself through university, I finally graduated and had to go out and find a job. Through my degree, I had specialised in biomedical science, and I did my six weeks of volunteer industry experience at a hospital, and to this day I would be happy to never set foot in one again.

I knew I could strike off working as a biomedical engineer from the list of potential jobs. There I was, an electronic engineer with a heap of specialisation in biomedical science, but I didn't want to work in that field, or electronics either. I had spent five years studying, but I was no closer to figuring out what I actually wanted to do.

In 2005 I applied for four jobs and managed to get three interviews. The first interview was with a power utility company, the second was for the role of mud engineer with an offshore drilling company based on chemical engineering, and the third was for a job in Perth as a biomedical-equipment salesman.

I was offered the job from the first interview. A few weeks later I started, fresh eyed and totally ignorant of what I was getting myself into. I spent the last of my savings on a few pairs of dress pants, shirts and ties. There was a mix-up with my first paycheque and I wasn't paid for six weeks, by which time I was flat broke and living on crumbs. I decided that living paycheque to paycheque sucked, and I vowed to never be in that position again.

After splashing out on an iPod and buying food, I put the rest into savings; month by month, my savings steadily increased.

Thankfully my girlfriend at the time, whom I met in my first year at university (and is now my wife), was on the same page as me. We saved diligently, and she was able to buy a new car a little over twelve months after starting work, and I was able to do the same shortly after. We've kept this saving habit going over the years, and have never had to borrow a cent to buy our vehicles.

It was around this time that I bought my first tranche of shares, a massive investment of $1,000. It didn't work out so well, but I learned important lessons from it.

Towards the end of my second year with the company, an opportunity came up for me to transfer to Brisbane to take on a project-coordinator role, so we made the move. I understood that the new role meant I would leave the graduate program, but when I arrived in Brisbane I was told that I was still on the program, and that I could kiss the $20,000 pay rise goodbye. A few months later I told my boss that if he couldn't find a $30,000 pay rise I would leave. He found the money and I stayed for another six months, before I was poached by an upcoming oil and gas company—for another $20,000 pay rise plus a 10-percent bonus on top if I performed.

During this time we purchased our first home. We put down a 30-percent deposit and had one goal: to pay off the mortgage as quickly as we could.

After three years it was time for me to move on. I had put out a few feelers in the market, and one day I received a job offer from one of the company's competitors. They offered me literally double my current salary to take on the role of project engineer for a high-voltage electrical scope on a mega project. It was a contractor role for an initial term of two years. There was no sick pay or annual leave; if I worked I got paid, as simple as that.

My wife and I discussed the risks of me taking up the role. We were in a fairly stable position: we were ahead of the mortgage and had put aside roughly six months of living expenses, so we decided to take the risk.

Soon after I took on the role, it was clear to me that the mega project had some significant issues. Within a few months I stepped into a managerial role and took on more people, and was subsequently promoted to lead. A rate review was done after I had been there for a year, and my manager went to bat for me in a big way. We submitted my performance review to HR, and I was later told that I would receive a 34-percent pay rise. My mind raced as I tried to calculate how much that equated to in dollar terms.

My two-year contract was extended by a year four times. I wasn't eligible for any further pay rises, partly due to the high pay I was already receiving but also because of the massive decline in oil prices during this time.

Working on this project, life was tough and intense. I was responsible for the safety of the crew in some high-risk situations, and adding to the stress were the budgets; these oil and gas facilities would generate millions of dollars in revenue each day.

My wife and I had made massive sacrifices to get ahead. By the time I was thirty-two we had paid off our house and were on our way to building a decent portfolio of shares. Learning lessons from early wins and some decent losses, we settled on our preferred investment strategy of lower-risk blue-chip shares that paid out reasonable dividends.

I'd always had the goal of retiring at the age of forty. When I told an older colleague that I wanted to retire at forty to do something I was more passionate about, he asked me what that was. I had zero idea. With that single question he had toppled my entire house of cards. I now had to find out exactly what I was passionate about.

Towards the end of the mega project things were tough. I was working massively long days, often away from home for ten days straight before being flown home for four days' R&R. We now had two children so I spent my four days at home playing with the kids, mowing the lawns, and preparing meals for the coming weeks to try to take the load off my exhausted wife—while still taking numerous work phone calls. I had zero downtime, and I ran on adrenaline for over twelve months. I was hardly sleeping, and was irritable and tired.

At this point I was in charge of a $50 million scope, and had around a hundred and fifty people reporting to me on site. They all needed me to be on my A-game to ensure the project was completed as efficiently as possible without anyone getting hurt.

At the end of the project, we ended up energising the high-voltage network about ten days ahead of schedule. Everything went according to plan, and the insurmountable pressure from upper management disappeared in an instant. I went from dealing with putting out spot fires all day every day, fending off management, protecting my team, and dealing with in excess of a hundred emails a day to having almost nothing to do. My emails dropped to ten per day. My crews all took much-needed time off, or were demobilised.

I sat there with nothing to do, but my brain was still spinning at a million miles an hour. I had completely burned out.

One night not long after this, I found I couldn't hold a can of Canadian Club because my hands were shaking so badly, and things spiralled downwards from there. I was offered a three-month extension to help out some other aspects of the project, but after three weeks

I couldn't stand it anymore. I quit without another job to go to, and ended up taking four months off to pick up the pieces.

During those four months I spent a lot of time contemplating my purpose in life and reading a lot of books. I ended up taking another 12-month contract with a different company, but I didn't have the energy to put my heart and soul into the job. Midway through this contract I went on an amazing retreat, where I came up with the idea of the Rapid Online Mentoring program.

Engineering and project management don't really lend themselves to helping people, but mentoring the younger members of my teams was something that had kept me going. Mentoring had become my outlet. I wanted to get into more one-on-one coaching, and I especially wanted to help younger graduates because they had the potential to create the greatest impact.

I had finally discovered my passion: I was passionate about mentoring. I wanted to ensure that the next generation reached their full potential, either by following in my footsteps or avoiding many of the pitfalls I had experienced. But most of all I wanted to ensure that the next generation lived a life of purpose, passion and prosperity in line with their own personal values and goals.

I took stock of everything that had happened in my life and owned it. I recognised that I did some things very well, but not other things. I looked at the areas I struggled with, and made improvements.

What have I learned from my experiences? After helping hundreds of younger graduates and team members, I now understand the pinch points that people have difficulty with. From these teachings, and my own experiences, I have produced the following guidelines to help you take your life and career further, faster.

ACKNOWLEDGEMENTS

To my wife and children: you are my world.
Thank you for everything you have brought to my life.
And a massive thanks to everyone who has helped in getting me
to this point; honestly, I couldn't have done it without you.

INTRODUCTION

A word of warning: *Further Faster* is not intended to be a thesis that references multiple case studies per point made. I've made every endeavour to make the book as short as possible while delivering as much value as possible.

With this in mind, I decided that offering multiple case studies or reference reports would take up too much space and time, so instead I have focused on high-value examples, referenced the original creator of content, and provided additional reading references where appropriate. I have condensed the information as much as possible to make my points. And I make many, many points throughout the book.

Throughout this book you will find QR codes which you can use to quickly access the online content I refer to at that point. Simply open your smart phone camera app and hover your phone over the code.

I make no apologies for the overabundance of knowledge and value contained in these pages. I trust that you will find *Further Faster* to be an invaluable source of knowledge, and that it will help you accelerate your life.

Achieving an amazing, stellar career together with a healthy, happy lifestyle may take some effort and may not always be easy, but it will be worth it. With a little hard work and dedication, together with a sense of passion and pride in what you do, you can reach your goals. Let me tell you that you can create your own plan, equip yourself with the tools required, and live the life you want.

I have engaged with countless people over the past fifteen years, and the common resounding factor that comes up time and time again is that most people don't have a plan. They have no idea where they want to get to in life; they're just floating around as if lost at sea—rudderless ships, if you will. This goes on until things reach breaking point and something has to give. They realise they're slaving away, just going through the motions while getting nowhere, a situation that can lead to a nervous breakdown or mid-life crisis.

By contrast, the highly successful, driven people of this world usually have a crystal-clear vision of their future and where they want to get to; they have goals and ambitions, and they strive to make their mark on the world.

Many people get lost in life and never seek to find their purpose. When they finally hit rock bottom or face a mid-life crisis, it requires countless hours of therapy or coaching to resolve, often costing thousands of dollars. For those in their forties and fifties, it can be a lot of effort unravelling the bad habits they have managed to weave into their daily lives. At the end of the arduous process they find that they have limited time left to lead purposeful, impactful lives—lives they never knew they wanted or needed—and often wish they had undertaken this journey much earlier.

Tackling some of these issues head on at the beginning of your career will give you the ultimate headstart. You can avoid the pitfalls and learn these hard life lessons the easy way. Life doesn't need to be an endless drift at sea with no destination in sight; you can create your own plan and strive for the greatness you know you can achieve. In essence, this is what this book is all about.

Further Faster is not your typical read-it-once-and-pass-it-on book. I encourage you to take your time reading through the pages. I believe that the information it contains is worth every minute you spend on it. Read at your own pace, multiple times if necessary, bookmark relevant sections, and revise at the right time for you.

For maximum benefit, I suggest you purchase a blank journal or notebook and keep it with this book. Make notes as you read, complete exercises from this book in your journal, doodle your thoughts when you encounter new ideas or stimulating material in your everyday activities. What you write, you are more likely to achieve.

Make a plan, work on it, review it, and come back and read the book again to adjust your plan along the way. No life plan should be fixed in stone. Life happens. Your wants, needs and values will all shift over time, and it's important that you are in tune with what you want from life at every stage. What you want in your twenties will likely be vastly different to what you want in your sixties, so it's important to think and plan for what you want from life when you reach your sixties while you're still in your twenties.

The rest of your life doesn't need to be a blank void of nothingness. You can and should create a plan for the future. Start with the end in mind and map out your own vision.

This book is dedicated to helping you determine your desired career goals, preparing you for the journey, and providing you with the tools and tips you need to accelerate your achievements and get there sooner.

Designing your ultimate life and career is an exercise in planning, preparation and execution. First, plan where you want to get to. This is your destination. Next, ensure you're completely prepared for the journey ahead. Finally, focus on execution: what you can put in place to make your journey as efficient, stress free and impactful as possible.

Life will invariably throw you curveballs and so your plan might need to change over time. It's important to remember that although you can't change the wind, you can adjust your sails. Turbulence is to be expected. It can be your friend, helping you build your own internal resilience and grit, and making you even more determined to reach for the stars.

To gain the full value from this book, you will need to do the work. Simply reading the content will deliver some value, but it will only be scratching the surface. Reading and absorbing the information will take you roughly six hours, and completing the challenges throughout the book will likely take you another ten hours. I am asking you now: please invest the full sixteen hours.

Here is your opportunity to dig your well before you get thirsty. Planning your life and career is much like planning a holiday to a set destination. You don't just go to the airport, jump on a plane and travel to a random destination. Instead, you decide on your destination *before* you leave. Only after you know where you're going do you start working on the steps to get there. You and you alone must set your own destination; it cannot be the result of someone else's desires.

It's absolutely crucial that you set goals to strive for, rather than going nowhere for years on end. Without proper planning I guarantee you will get lost, make mistakes, and rob yourself of great opportunities. There will be setbacks, curveballs and brick walls to go over, under or around. This book will help you develop resilience to these setbacks and work on your mindset to set your gaze for the stars.

Further Faster is divided into three parts.

In the first part, titled Plan Your Journey, you will take a deep dive into who you are and where you want to go. What is your ultimate destination? What obstacles will you need to overcome to get there?

Once you have planned your journey, you will need to pack your bags with the required equipment and tools.

The second part of the book, Pack Your Bags, will give you all the information you need to do this. This is where things get interesting. You will find some great advice about things that everyone struggles with. This section is loaded with effective tools you might never have known about, and lessons that can't be learned in school, university, or from your employer. These are the life lessons that everyone learns, often the hard way.

The third part, Accelerate Your Journey, discusses the ways in which you can work smarter to perform better, and get to your destination quicker, with fewer setbacks along the way. This section is where you will learn how to become a high performer.

PART 1
PLAN YOUR JOURNEY

CHAPTER 1

Find Direction in Life

I often meet people who are struggling with their careers, and they all say very similar things. *I don't know what I'm doing. I feel like a rudderless ship bobbing around at sea.* The variety of reasons people give for feeling confused is endless, and they all point to a common lack of direction in their lives.

I have coined a new expression: the I-dunno generation. Regardless of the questions I ask, I seem to get only one answer: *I dunno*. Where do you want to work? *I dunno*. What do you want from life? *I dunno*. What's on your bucket list? *I dunno*.

I hope you gain some insight from reading this book and start coming up with a few other answers for yourself. This is your life; don't waste it.

Firstly, let's take a look at the average person's take on their direction in life:

- Primary school: *I want to be a fireman/actress/nurse.*
- Secondary school: *I have no idea what I want to be when I get older.*
- End of secondary school: *I like cars so I'll become a mechanic. I did okay in maths and physics so I'll study engineering. My mum and dad are lawyers so I'll study law.*
- Finishing university: *I have no idea where I want to work so I'll take the first job that's offered to me.*
- Throughout career: *I have no idea where I want to get to or what I want to achieve.*
- Retirement: *I think I might go travelling and reminisce on all the lost opportunities.*

A wasted life means not actually considering where you want to go, or what you want to achieve. It can also mean knowing what you want but not having the guts to go after it. This section of the book is all about contemplating the purpose of your life, who you are, where you want to go, what you want to be remembered for, and the legacy you want to leave behind. Using our travel metaphor from the introduction, you need to choose your destination and pick the routes you could take to get there.

As with any great adventure, you must set the scene by looking at where you are now. Who are you as a person? What is your personality type? What are your values? What makes you tick? What stresses you out? What are your fears? What motivates you? What drives you? Learn more about yourself, hone your mindset, and develop your resilience.

Even if you have already undertaken some of the following psychometric tests, I encourage you to repeat them. As with all psychometric testing, the results can change depending on your mindset, mood and environment at the time of testing. This variance should be less than ten percent, but it will change slightly over time.

There are some simple ways you can find out all about yourself, so follow along with the activities. Each of these taken in isolation is okay, but if you combine them, that's when the results become really useful.

PERSONALITY TESTS

The Myers-Briggs personality-type indicator has been one of the go-to personality tests since it was invented by American mother/daughter duo Katherine Cook Briggs and Isabel Briggs Myers. The test itself was developed during World War Two and first published in 1944. Considering that neither Myers nor Briggs were trained psychologists (both were trained in psychometric testing) the test has attracted its fair share of criticism from psychology purists. Although I'm not a psychologist either, I think the test provides great personal insight and can help you understand who you are.

You can complete the personality test free online (www.16personalities.com). The results will tell you if your personality leans toward extroversion (E) or introversion (I), sensing (S) or intuition (N), thinking (T) or feeling (F), and judgment (J) or perception (P).

Use this QR code to access the 16 Personalities website.

What does all this really mean? For a start, you can learn a lot about yourself. It can show you if you're more likely to be outspoken or shy in social environments—although that doesn't mean that if you're an introvert you won't succeed at public speaking. After all, social confidence also plays a massive part.

I have had a lot of success with the 16 Personalities website (www.16personalities.com), which delivers a report that will help you understand more about your results. I believe the 16 Personalities test is useful and I encourage you to take it.

Personality types also have a great deal to do with energy levels. Introverts can become exhausted and drained by being in loud social environments. Extroverts, on the other hand, thrive in and get pumped up by these situations.

Does any of this sound familiar to you? Perhaps this will come in handy when you're managing a team. Reflect on your own personality type and try to gather strategies to work to your strengths. If you're introverted and are attending a busy all-day workshop, remember to take time to be alone occasionally and recharge your energy levels.

'I have learned I can survive just about anything so long as I am occasionally allowed a few quiet moments to myself—time to restore my spirit, to mend my wounds, to regroup. A little me time and I can deal with anything the world sends my way.'

—BEAU TALPIN

VALUES

Now we'll take a look at your personal values, a process that can give you insight into what you believe deep down at your core. The online tool on the Barrett Values Centre website (www.valuescentre.com/tools-assessments/pva/) will help you identify your personal values in a free values assessment. From this, you will gain insight into what your personal values are. There are some insightful activities to work through in the values-assessment report.

Use this QR code to access the values assessment tool.

Once you know what your values are you will find it much easier to understand why some things grate on you. For instance, you'll be able to understand why you intuitively don't trust someone you meet; chances are it's because your values don't align with the other person's. I encourage you to use the values-assessment tools, check your results, and take a deep dive into changing or modifying any limiting values you identify. Completing this values assessment will help to define what is important to you at this point in your life.

You will have picked up many of your values during your childhood from your parents or primary caregivers. Your parents/caregivers will have passed on their values and their idea of what is right or wrong. Undertaking a values assessment at this point in your life will allow you to assess which values have come from others, and which are yours alone. From this, you can assess which ones you want to hold onto, and which you want to work towards changing.

In early childhood you're a blank slate and rely on your parents for survival; you accept their values and make them your own; however, when you become an adult you can make a conscious choice to either live by your parents' values or choose values that are better suited to you. Unfortunately, a misalignment can occur if you continue to hold onto values that are no longer a good fit for your life.

For example, let's say your parents had a strong work ethic. They valued hard work and didn't believe in taking time off to relax. You, however, choose to work a regular workweek and employ a cleaner to help out around the house. In this scenario, you might experience an underlying feeling of guilt that you should always be doing something, and find it hard to relax on the weekends.

If you can recognise that there is a mismatch between your own and your parents' work values, this understanding will reduce any feelings of guilt, or what psychologists refer to as cognitive dissonance (doing something that conflicts with your values).

Many people's values are determined by both the culture in which they live and the circumstances of their lives. Your parents' values are likely to be a combination of how they were brought up and societal influences on their lives. The world has changed dramatically over the past thirty years or so, and not all previous values are as important now. Take, for example, the generation that lived through the Great Depression. The attitude of this generation towards work and life will be very different from your view of work and life.

Early in your career, it's perfectly natural for you to have quite a few values in the survival zone. This is a reflection of the values you have when you're in the process of establishing yourself and seeking security. However, once you've become successfully established, you will probably find that your confidence and self-esteem grow, and your values shift.

The goal is for you to shift the balance of your values from the survival zone towards transformation, ending with a healthy spread across the board. While it's totally acceptable to have some values in the survival zone, you need to identify the potentially limiting values in this area and make a conscious choice not to embody them.

Ultimately, values are all about what matters to *you*. They may change over time, maybe even significantly, and you may even find them changing as you work through this book.

Before doing the test, I encourage you to take a deep breath and try to relax as much as possible. Don't overthink your answers too much, and don't try to second-guess them, trying to figure out what will look good or bad. The more honest your answers are, the more you can learn from the experience. You are the only one who needs to see the results. What you do with these results is up to you.

Knowing your core values will allow you to align your work to your values. Ask yourself how your job can help you meet your values. Travel might be one of your core values, in which case your job can provide you with the financial means required to travel the world.

For more practical examples of finding your core values and aligning your life to these, I recommend you read *The Values Factor* by Dr John Demartini.

By now you should be starting to get a fairly good idea of what makes you who you are. Would you believe that you're not even halfway there yet? Let's take a look at what the other half looks like.

WHAT YOU ARE CAPABLE OF

Have you ever contemplated what you, as an individual, are capable of? Depending on your personality and self-beliefs, you may be selling yourself short due to underlying negative core beliefs.

Believing that you're not capable of achieving something will pretty well cement in place the conviction that you won't achieve it. If, on the other hand, you believe deep down that one day you could achieve something, that faint glimmer of hope can give you the confidence to try, fail, get up and try again, and one day succeed in achieving your goal.

Sit down somewhere peaceful and scribble down on a notepad all the things you think you're capable of achieving in your lifetime. I personally love when these capabilities become less about the individual and more about serving others. You could include leaving a legacy or working with charities. These things will all be closely aligned with your values. This can be a tricky exercise, so give it some time. Give yourself permission to dream; allow yourself to transcend your current situation in life.

Write down your own list of capabilities, both as they are now and what they could be in the future. Believe in your ability to achieve your goals in life.

For now, focus on the four pillars listed on the next page (each pillar will be discussed in depth in the coming chapters). Using your notebook, start to drop some ideas under each with regard to what you think you're capable of. Here are a few examples to get you started:

- Career
    - Earn $100,000 per year before retirement
    - Reach department-manager level

- Finances
    - Save a 10-percent house deposit in two years
    - Retire at sixty-five, self-funded

- Bucket list
    - Visit the pyramids
    - Cook for the homeless at Christmas

- Personal life
    - Go on a yoga retreat
    - Learn to meditate

What if you were to expand, embellish or even double your capabilities? Let's say you had a personal capability of earning $100,000 per year. What would it take to increase this amount by ten percent? What would it take to double this amount? Which areas would you need to develop to do that? What would it take to earn this much through investments so you never needed to work again?

Consider what would happen if you accelerated these capabilities? For example, let's say you want to earn $100,000 by the age of thirty-five. Let's take another look at the list of your capabilities with that example in mind:

- Career
    - ~ Earn $100,000 per year ~~before retirement~~ *by age thirty-five*
    - ~ Reach department manager level *by age forty*

- Finances
    - ~ Save a ~~10-percent~~ *20-percent* house deposit in two years
    - ~ Retire at ~~sixty-five~~ *fifty-five* self-funded

- Bucket list
    - ~ Visit the pyramids *and do a helicopter tour*
    - ~ Cook for the homeless at Christmas *this year*

- Personal life
    - ~ Go on a yoga retreat *in Bali*
    - ~ Learn to meditate *this year*

Try to expand your own opinion of yourself. You're better than you believe, and it may only be your mindset that's holding you back. You can achieve great things when you put your mind, heart and soul into them.

YOU ARE ENOUGH

There is a growing trend towards the belief that, as individuals, we're not good enough. This internal core belief comes from many, many societal influences, and while it's quite prevalent it can have a catastrophic impact on each person's ability to reach their full potential. It is generally shown as low self-esteem, and researching the statistics is frightening. For example, would you believe that according to the *Huffington Post,* four out of five women suffer from low self-regard?

Social media is a massive contributor to this trend, and is full of people posting pictures of how perfect their lives are. *Look at me, I'm on holiday and I've just had a spray tan.* People instinctively want to show off and portray themselves as being rich and successful. The truth is that many of today's so-called 'influencers' are doing nothing more than faking it, for example, renting cars they then show off on social media. Some people who are flaunting their wealth and status may be genuine, but they may still only be telling half the story—the half they want you to see.

Have you ever held yourself back from doing something? For instance, not introduced yourself to that person, not applied for that promotion, not put your hand up to ask that question. All because you had a feeling deep down that you weren't good enough, or didn't deserve the outcome you hoped for. More than ninety-five percent of the population feels a lack of self-esteem from time to time, so you're not alone. This lack of confidence can also be shown through embarrassment, which stems largely from caring too much what other people think. Caring more about what others think than achieving your own goals is a surefire way to achieve nothing.

Alternatively, you might experience discomfort when stepping outside your comfort zone. You may feel like there's a shadow looming overhead, following your every move. Or you may have a simple fear that you will one day be found out as a fraud who doesn't know what they're doing.

Some of the causes of a deep-seated belief that you're not enough are: upbringing; parents who were never supportive enough; friends or family members who have constantly put you down; societal attitudes in general, that seem to imply that if you don't have enough experience you're not worthy; and all the way down to social media and the constant barrage of messaging that *my life is better than yours*.

Believing you're enough is a huge leveller in life. It will shed a massive weight from your shoulders and allow you to step outside your comfort zone with ease and confidence. Here are a few great tips for shifting from a not-enough mindset to an enough mindset:

- Ask yourself how you would act if you were enough. You can act this way now.
- What would you say to someone if you thought you were enough? You can say this right now.
- Picture yourself being enough. Maybe you're up on stage giving a presentation, or asking questions, or talking to a particular person, or taking that new role, or taking a leap of faith.
- Focus on all the ways that you're already enough. Rather than listing all the reasons why you're *not* qualified for the promotion, list all the reasons why you are. Reframe the negativity into optimistic ways you can conquer a problem.
- Practise gratitude on a daily basis.
- Repeat affirmations telling yourself that you are enough. I also recommend that you watch a video by Marisa Peer, who has coined the term 'statements of truth', which refers to repeatedly telling yourself, 'I am enough'. (https://marisapeer.com/smillion-mori-marisa-peer/)

Use this QR code to access the Marisa Peer video.

Each and every day we tell ourselves all kinds of negative things: *I can't remember names. I can't climb that hill. I don't know how to do that.* Note that all of these statements are final. The more often you tell yourself you can't do something, the more you will believe it and the less likely it is you will achieve it.

One very effective solution is to add the word *yet* onto the end of your sentences. *I can't remember names yet. I can't climb that hill yet. I don't know how to yet.* By adding *yet* you're telling yourself there is hope that one day in the future you will be able to do it. It injects hope and instantly adjusts your gaze from looking downwards to looking upwards.

It might not happen overnight, but it might surprise you how quickly success does come along with the right *yet* mindset. Simply changing the way you think will have a massive impact on your chances of success.

If you really struggle to shake this mindset, I recommend you consider seeing a psychologist. Shifting this mindset will open up your future to so many possibilities. Psychologists are not just trained in treating mental illness like anxiety, depression and so on; they have a profound ability to shift problematic mindsets as well.

While we're on the topic of psychologists, have a think about your own mental wellbeing. Do you have any baggage that you don't want to carry for the rest of your life? If you're susceptible to any sort of mental illness such as depression, anxiety or negativity, or if you have a negative self-belief, the best time to have this addressed is right now. Taking care of your mind is incredibly important, and the benefits can be out of this world if you get the appropriate treatment. Please don't wait until you're in your later years to address any concerns; you will only be cheating yourself of the time between now and then.

Not everyone will want to take my advice on this one, but I'm willing to bet that twenty years from now you'll be wishing you had. Do your future self a favour: be brave and seek therapy if you think you need it. Do it for yourself and those around you.

Now we'll move onto building up the four pillars that are going to support you for the rest of your life.

CHAPTER 2

Four Pillars

There are four distinct pillars that you need to focus on when you're framing your future. These pillars form the foundation of your best possible life. I strongly believe that if you put ample focus on each one, great things will come into your life.

The four key pillars:

PERSONAL LIFE

CAREER GOALS

BUCKET LIST

FINANCES

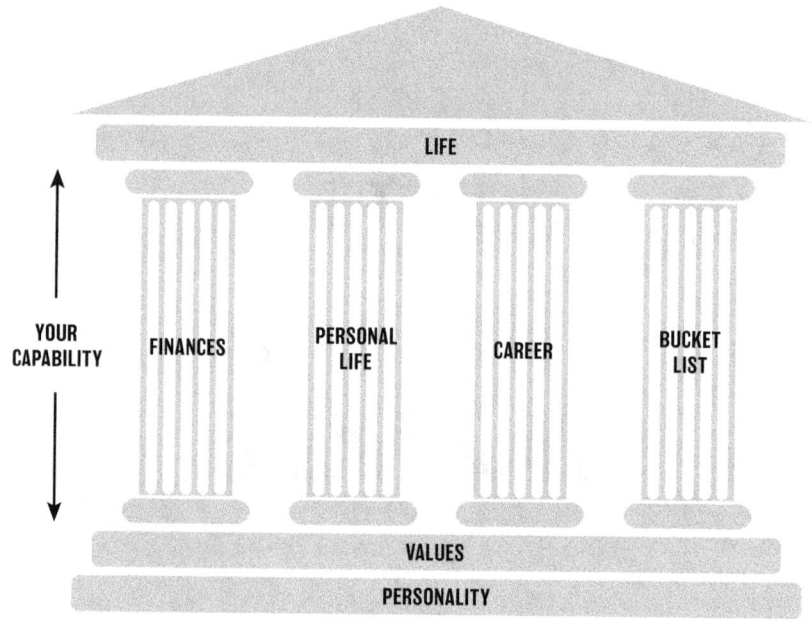

The four pillars form a foundation on which you can build an amazing life. When you find the right balance between the pillars you'll start to find the interconnectedness between them. Your career will in turn help to boost your finances. Having your finances in order will allow you to tick off your wildest bucket-list items. And achieving the goals set out in your bucket list will enhance your personal life.

Your improved personal life will allow you to relax in your downtime, allowing you to head back to work refreshed and energised, and ready to put in the work. Chasing career opportunities for much higher salaries is not easy if you don't have a cash buffer.

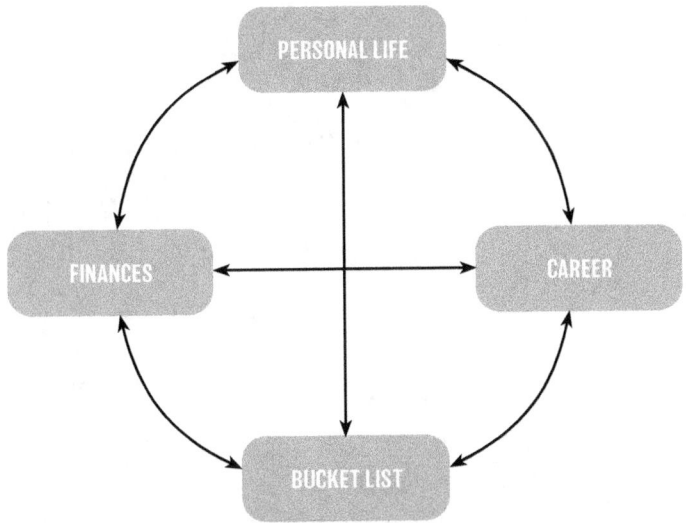

    These four pillars form the structure of your life. If one fails, there can be a lack of balance, or the entire structure might even come crashing down. As you can see, a lack of order in your finances will force you to play it safe with your career. A lower earning capacity will lead to more stress in your personal life, and disappointment when you can't tick off your bucket-list items. A sub-par personal life will impact on your ability to perform at your peak in your career.

    Balance is the key here. The structure of your life can be as tall and grand as you like, as long as you find balance between these pillars. If your spending habits outpace your career and financial abilities, you will run up unimaginable debts, and we all know the consequences of that.

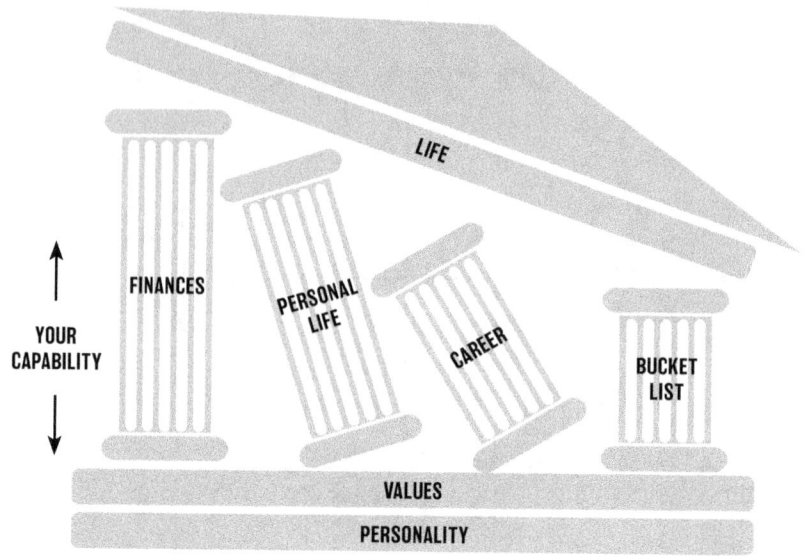

PERSONAL LIFE

Your personal life is everything that happens outside of work: it includes where you live, whom you interact with, what you eat, and so much more. The most important thing I can say about living the personal life you want to live is *do it on your own terms.*

Be fully aware of the con that is social media. Be aware that people you follow only share the things they are most proud of. Honestly, the grass isn't greener on the other side of the fence, and if you want the grass to be greener on your side you need to *water it.*

Consider what your ultimate personal life would look like. Here are a few possibilities:

- More friends than you can count *or* a few quality mates
- A lifestyle of eating out *or* cooking for friends and family
- Travelling the globe *or* exploring your own backyard

- Training to compete in an Ironman triathlon *or* joining your local surf club
- Living in a mansion on the beach *or* living in a cosy neighbourhood
- Downtown CBD *or* the wilderness
- Going out clubbing *or* having a quiet night in with friends

There's so much to consider. I could go on and on, but the point is to chase what you really want, not what will impress your friends, family, or the followers you have on Instagram (that you don't even know). Your personal life needs a certain blend of friends, exercise, hobbies and other things that bring meaning to your life.

Meditation is another valuable tool to add to your list, an activity that's well worth practising. The *Cambridge Dictionary* definition for meditation: 'The act of giving your attention to only one thing.' Meditation can take many forms. In the past I have called these various options 'alternate meditation', where you simply do something you enjoy, something that makes you lose all sense of time, where your mind is focused purely on that one thing. It could be fishing, sunbaking on the beach, gardening, or even extreme sports.

Riding dirt bikes has always been my personal meditation. Helmet on = brain off. Okay, not literally brain off, more an absolute focus and concentration on what I'm doing. Extreme sports provide the adrenaline rush of getting away with near-death experiences, and while this is a thrill-seeking rush, it's also an intense form of meditation.

What is your alternate meditation, and how often do you practise it? You might find that if you do it a little more often you'll see an elevation in your mood and general sense of wellbeing. If you can't get out and do your preferred alternate meditation, check out the Insight Timer app and slip on the headphones for a little more traditional guided meditation.

'A mind may be likened to a garden, which may be intelligently cultivated or allowed to run wild; but whether cultivated or neglected, it must, and will bring forth. If no useful seeds are put into it, then an abundance of useless weed seeds will fall therein, and will continue to produce their kind.'

—JAMES ALLEN

This is a striking quote from James Allen. Consider your own mind. What weeds are growing, and what beautiful flowers are present that you never pay attention to? It's time to take stock of what's growing in your mind, and pull out or poison the weeds. In their place plant new seeds of traits you wish to develop and water over time. With observation and the right nurturing, you can turn your mind into a beautiful garden.

Your internal thoughts and mind chatter really do have an impact on your outward appearance, how you act and who you are as a person. Practising self-care is a crucial skill to master. Any time you're beating yourself up over something, it's important to recognise what you're doing and change those thoughts.

One such theory surrounds the term *automatic negative thoughts* (ANTs). Consider that your thoughts can be classified as either positive or negative. The human brain has what is called a negativity bias. This is an evolutionary function designed to keep us safe. Our minds are always looking for the worst in any situation and trying to avoid previous pain points.

One way you can overcome these ANTs is to become a master of reframing. Whenever a particular thought comes up that has a negative connotation, try to reframe the thought into a positive. For example, rather than wondering why something negative happened to you, consider what you learned from that situation. If you're dealing with someone you don't like or have had bad dealings with in the past, try to be positive in the next encounter and thank them for their assistance. You never know, your approach may just mend a burned bridge and make your life easier in the future. (I cover some further reframing exercises in the coming chapters.)

'Your beliefs become your thoughts,
Your thoughts become your words,
Your words become your actions,
Your actions become your habits,
Your habits become your values,
Your values become your destiny.'
—MAHATMA GHANDI

List your top ten personal life goals and roughly what age you want to be when you achieve them:

	PERSONAL LIFE GOALS	AGE
1		
2		
3		
4		
5		
6		
7		
8		
9		
10		

CAREER GOALS

I spent close to fifteen years working my way up the corporate ladder, struggling for the most part and never quite feeling like everything was working for me. I was constantly stressed and anxious, and I didn't enjoy the work I was doing or the industries I worked in. I never enjoyed the day-to-day aspects of what I was doing and constantly felt out of my element.

I was getting paid well—very well—and this spurred me on for a long time. For many years I worked for nothing more than the salary I received, but the work I did was only ever satisfying retrospectively. It soon became apparent to me that I wasn't working in line with my personal values, and my work life was actually *clashing* with many of these personal values. Work was dragging me away from my family, requiring me to deal with conflict on a daily basis, and stifling my creative nature.

Ikigai, pronounced 'ee-key-guy', is a simple and enlightening Japanese concept that has resonated with me. The word is formed from two Japanese words—*iki*, meaning life, and *gai*, meaning effect. Bridged together, they effectively become *life meaning* or *reason for being*, and illustrate how and why a particular aspect of your life may feel out of balance. For a long time—even though I was falling strongly into the space of being comfortable on the ikigai chart below—I had a feeling of emptiness, largely because I was not doing something I loved.

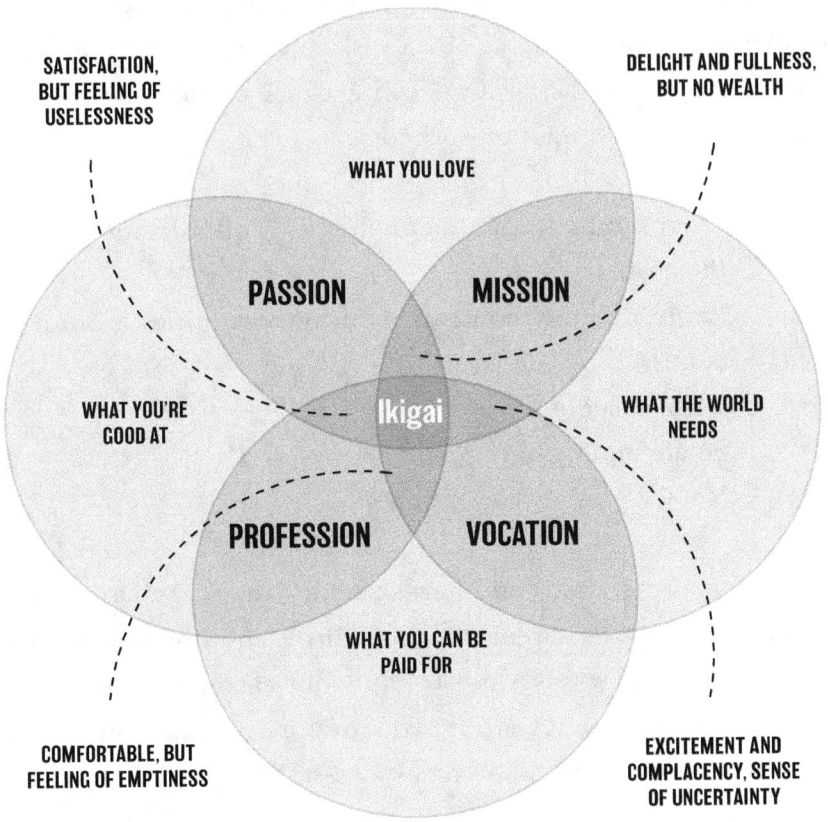

I strongly recommend that you study the chart. I have seen countless similar versions, but this is the only one that actually makes sense to me, with real emotional examples of how you feel in each segment.

Take some time to search online for the concept. There is some enlightening information out there about exploring this concept and it can help in those times when you're not feeling fulfilled.

What are your career goals, aspirations, dream roles? Do you want to climb the corporate ladder all the way to the top, or is middle management your goal? Whatever your personal career goals are, write them down and start making plans to achieve them. You may find that you reach them faster than you would have thought possible, leaving room to set new, even more ambitious goals. Regardless of your level of experience, you should be able to ask yourself some key questions to help figure this out. Start by deciding which of the following types of organisations you want to work for:

- Large multinational company with opportunities across the globe
- Large national company with opportunities around the country
- Local small business
- Small family-run business
- Not-for-profit organisation

Grab your notebook and start sketching out ideas. Do you want a lifestyle career or a career lifestyle? This is an important decision to make. In other words, do you want your career to support your lifestyle, or do you want your lifestyle to support your career? Either answer is perfectly fine. Some very successful people have their lives rotate around their careers. Other successful people fit their careers around their lives. How you define success or happiness is up to you. Try asking yourself the following questions:

- Do you want to manage other people?
- Do you want to work with technology or with your hands?
- Do you want to be indoors or outdoors?
- Do you want to lead an organisation?

Only by asking yourself these questions, and many others, can you start to define what you want from your career.

In most professions, workers can transition through three main phases. When starting out, almost everyone will start with a technician role. The technician is the person on the ground who does the actual work. After becoming sufficiently experienced, the technician can make the transition to a manager role, and become the person who *manages* the technicians. Not everyone will make this transition. Many people are happy to stay in a technician role for their entire careers, and there are many examples of people achieving amazing results doing exactly that.

The final step beyond the manager role is the leader, the person responsible for the outlook of the company on a timeframe of one to five years. Again, not all managers will transition to leaders.

Deciding where you aspire to reach in these stages can help you gain clarity over your desired career path. Again, there are no right or wrong answers.

Spend some time thinking about your ultimate career goals. Once you have a fair idea of the level you want to reach within an industry, an effective way to start plotting your course to your desired level is to obtain a copy of your company's organisation chart (you may need to ask HR for a copy).

On your copy of the chart, put a big red circle around the position that is your career goal. Keep in mind that this is *your* goal and no one else's. *You* decide how far up or down the ladder you want to go. Not everyone wants or needs to climb to the top of the corporate ladder.

Now for the fun part: playing snakes and ladders. If you take a look at your goal career position and the skill sets required to fulfil such a position, you can start to build a list of personal-development training you need to undertake to reach this spot. Some types of training will come from fulfilling roles, others will come from external training, mentoring or even self-managed learning.

Now take some time to plot the various paths you could take from your current position to your goal position. This may not always be a straight path upwards. You may want to consider taking sideways steps to gain exposure in different departments. Moving around the company can help to give you a foundation, and also a better sense of what the company does and how it operates.

As a word of caution, avoid sharing your desires with the person who is currently in the position you are aiming for. They may take offense at you gunning for their role and put barriers in place to protect themselves, effectively stifling your progress.

Take note of the skills gap between where you are now and where you want to be. Make a list of those shortages, and beside each one write down the ways in which you will obtain the necessary skills. For example, you might need exposure to finance and accounting, so your options could include spending time on secondment in the relevant department, or undertaking external training.

Not everyone wants to become the CEO of the company. Remember, the CEO reports to the board and the board reports to the shareholders. Just because you're sitting at the top of the tree doesn't mean you don't answer to anyone. For many, the level of responsibility that comes with sitting at the top of the tree can be daunting. There can be legal implications involved, public speaking, interviews, and episodes of fierce grilling when things go wrong.

Ultimately, you need to keep in mind the fundamental question: Do you want a lifestyle career or a career lifestyle?

Many people are more than happy just doing the work and have no interest in managing people. Again, remember the three main phases you can go through in your working career.

1. The technician (does the work)
2. The manager (manages the technicians)
3. The leader (guides the direction of the company and the people)

In many circumstances, in both large and small organisations, career progression can be extremely slow, and the only way to progress is to leave and join another company. Personally, I always see leaving as a last alternative. Sure, you may get that promotion that takes you outside your comfort zone, but changing companies comes with its own headaches. Changing companies means learning all new systems, new faces and names, and adapting to new organisational political systems. If you can ascend the ladder within your current employment, it's often the least stressful route.

I never wanted to reach the heights of being CEO. I didn't care for standing in front of the entire company to give a speech. I didn't care to be interviewed by reporters, and nor did I want to be personally responsible for the health and wellbeing of so many employees. Ultimately, I wanted to be as well-off financially as the CEO, but have a much better work-life balance. I wanted to have a lifestyle career, where I had enough spare time to manage my finances, make smart investments and, unlike many CEOs and top-tier executives, stay happily married to my wife (and not lose fifty percent of my wealth through divorce).

Another option can be to become friends with someone from the HR department and learn all about the world of human resources. Knowing how to effectively manage the three P's (people, personalities and politics) can be a crucial piece of the puzzle to master (more on this later).

Use the following table to list your top ten career goals, and roughly what age you want to be when you achieve them. It's of the utmost importance that you reflect on your answers and make sure you write down what *you* want. If you are doing things simply to impress others, that needs to stop now. Your career aspirations need to serve *you* and no one else.

	CAREER GOALS	AGE
1		
2		
3		
4		
5		
6		
7		
8		
9		
10		

BUCKET LIST

There are no golden rules for developing a bucket list. Everyone is different, so no two people will have exactly the same bucket-list desires. With that in mind, where do you begin? It's a good idea to start near the beginning of your life, so go back as far as you can remember.

I can hear you asking what a bucket list has to do with your career. Remember back at the start of the book when I said I was going to take your life and career further faster? I firmly believe that in order to achieve greatness in your career, your personal life needs to follow suit.

All the best leaders in the world take care of themselves, and having a bucket list is one aspect of this. Another important advantage of a bucket list is that it means you have outside-of-work experiences that give you reason to be compassionate towards your staff. A bucket list also gives you the motivation to keep pushing your career to new heights, which in turn enables you to gain more experiences.

So grab your journal or device and jot down your ideas for your bucket list. Here are a few ideas for fleshing out your list:

- What you wanted to be when you grew up: Chances are there might be some kind of lifelong yearned-for experience sitting in the back of your mind. Perhaps you wanted to be Maverick from *Top Gun* and fly a fighter jet, but life got in the way and you ended up as a scientist. This doesn't mean you can't experience a fighter-jet flight; from around $1500 you can co-pilot in a fighter jet, or experience a full-blown simulator for under $500.
- Favourite childhood movies: You might have a yearning to visit the places that were featured in those movies. Fans of Harry Potter might long for a trip to Alnwick Castle in the United Kingdom, while fans of *The Hobbit* may desire a trip to Middle Earth (New Zealand).
- Places you dream of visiting: If you could go anywhere in the world, where would you choose? Visiting Disneyland was a lifelong dream for a friend of mine, and she was thirty when she finally got to go.
- People you want to meet: In addition to individuals you'd like to meet, there might be sporting teams you want to watch play on their home ground, or shows or performers you want to see. A few years back I got to see the LA Lakers play in their home stadium. Is there a player you want to see before they retire?
- Physical endeavours you want to achieve: This could mean surfing the big waves in Hawaii, or running a marathon.

Bucket lists are not just lists of destinations. Try to consider them as things you want to do, see, feel, achieve or experience, so break it down into the following five categories. I've listed some examples of what you can include in each one:

- Things you want to do (feed the homeless on Christmas day, eat a chili dog at a Yankees game)
- Places you want to see (Machu Picchu)
- Things you want to feel (the wind in your face while you're skydiving)
- Things you want to achieve (become the CEO of the company, start your own business)
- Things you want to experience (do indoor rock-climbing, go to major concerts, see your favourite bands)

Once you've defined a list it's important that you embellish each idea, create a vision for it and write a sentence about it. For example, rather than just saying *Visit the pyramids* you could say *Enjoy Egypt on a Nile cruise, with a helicopter flight over the pyramids followed by exploring Tutankhamen's tomb.* Adding these extra details will bring life to each bucket-list item and cement the vision in your mind, powerfully motivating you to actually achieve them. If you have time, make a storyboard and embellish your items with pictures, which can be a visual pull to bring those goals to life.

Remember, this is *your* list so put down only those items that are for *you*. This is not a shopping list for ways to impress your friends or family. List your top ten bucket-list items and roughly what age you want to be when you complete them:

	BUCKET LIST ITEMS	AGE
1		
2		
3		
4		
5		
6		
7		
8		
9		
10		

Now it's time for a challenge. I want you to choose one short-term item from your list and put a plan in place to make it happen *this month*. You will thank me for this after you have done it. Sometimes all you need is a push. Put the book down, get out your notepad and start listing a few ideas for things you could tackle this month. Once you've chosen something, lock it in; make the booking.

FINANCES

The following information is general in nature and is not intended as financial advice, but it should give you an insight into what I have done and the personal path I have followed. Your own personal circumstances will of course be different.

Taking charge of your finances is a crucial step in setting yourself up for the future. It's so much harder to follow your dreams if you're broke; after all, the only reason I was able to write this book was because I had the financial freedom to do it.

It isn't easy being broke. Being broke sucks, and most of us have known what that's like at some stage of our lives. This is why it's so important to put steps in place to establish and protect your financial security. Once you've done that, you can stop worrying about money.

Towards the end of my university degree I made a strategic decision to stop working part-time so I could focus all my efforts on my final-semester studies, exams and thesis. The plan nearly backfired when I cut things a little too close. I knew the money would start coming in at some point, but I didn't factor in the need to buy clothes and other necessities. After that experience I vowed never to live paycheque to paycheque again.

Living with no savings is part of many people's lives, and can lead to them maxing out their credit cards and paying unnecessary interest. But with a little self-discipline, many people could get ahead of their finances and stash away a small cash buffer, which would remove so much stress and anxiety from their lives.

Countless surveys have shown that financial stress is one of the largest contributors to relationship breakdown and divorce. There may be times when a family's finances will be stretched, but I believe that with the right mindset, and the commitment to live within their means (spending less than they earn), many people could live with a whole lot less financial stress.

It's imperative that you're on the same financial page as your partner. There's no point having one person saving so the other can blow it, which will only lead to resentment and frustration down the track. Make sure you have a common financial goal. Make sure you talk about money together. If you're planning on spending the rest of your life with this person, you need to get your finances right, and the sooner the better.

Savings binge

If you're really struggling to get ahead of your finances, consider trying a savings binge for two months. Mark out the next two months of your calendar. During this time, try to avoid any unnecessary spending as much as possible, including going out for dinner. Eat at home, and cook enough for lunches the following day. Get creative with any presents you need to buy. Do whatever you can to save as much money as you possibly can, while still paying your bills and any other necessary expenditure.

It may help if you look at a typical month's expenditure and put every dollar you spend into a spreadsheet. If you're living paycheque to paycheque, this will almost certainly add up to your entire take-home salary. You might like to download the priority budget tool from the Rapid Online Mentoring website (https://rapidmentoring.com.au/bookresources/).

Use this QR code to access the Rapid priority budget tool.

In your expenditure spreadsheet, rank every item in order of priority. Put the most important items at the top, like food, rent and bills. Then work your way down to the least important items, like Netflix, gambling or Friday-night cocktails. Using this prioritised list you should be able to draw a survival line somewhere in the middle. Items above the line are crucial to your survival; items below the line are simply nice things to have.

This exercise will make you think about where you're spending your money. You need to make saving a priority and for it to be the first item below your survival line. Save your money before you waste it on meaningless clutter.

I did this exercise myself before stepping away from the corporate world to pursue my entrepreneurial career. I needed to make sure that my family was able to survive before I took the plunge.

Work out how much you are paid

Another revealing exercise is to determine how much you are actually paid. Knowing this can be a game changer. Once you can accurately calculate how many hours you would need to work to buy a particular item, your spending habits will change forever.

Your actual salary could be an impressive amount, say $70,000 per year. This is a big number, and it can fool people into thinking that they can afford anything.

To work out what your take-home amount is:

1. Look at your recent payslip and find the amount you were paid *after* deductions (tax, superannuation, etc).
2. Divide your take-home amount by the number of days worked in that pay cycle to get your day rate.
3. Divide your day rate by your nominated work hours (i.e. 7.6 hours) to get your take-home hourly rate.

Take-home pay_____/ **hours worked**_____ = **Rate $**_____ /hr

Put emotion into this equation. You know how hard you have to work to earn an hour of pay. Once you've compared your spending habits to your hours worked, you'll start questioning your spending habits. When you can sit back and say you have to work X number of hours to pay for a particular item, you can ask yourself how badly you need it.

This is when your spending habits will change. It's like knowing how many calories are in a chocolate bar versus how many hours you need to spend on the treadmill to work it off.

Take control of your finances

Don't go broke trying to look rich. Many people believe that money is the root of all evil and that greed corrupts the population. The Pareto Principle states that eighty percent of effects come from twenty percent of causes. Adapting this principle to a financial model, it has been shown that the wealthiest twenty percent earn over eighty percent of the world's income.

These statistics get worse if we look at the extreme ends of the wealth-distribution curve. According to the 2019 Credit Suisse Annual Global Wealth Report, in some segments of the world GDP (gross domestic product; one measure of economic activity), the bottom sixty percent of people earns just 5.74 percent of the world's gross income. The top 0.9 percent now owns almost fifty percent of the world's wealth. With these statistics in mind, it's easy to see how some people see a problem with the capitalistic nature of the Western world. While I can see their point (and there are many examples of this), it's preferable to look at the opportunities money can bring you:

- Money for survival: housing, food and basic needs
- Ability to follow your dreams
- Gaining experiences: travel, expanding your horizons through

- study, personal development
- Finding and pursuing your purpose in life
- Giving to those more in need
- Providing a better life for your family and loved ones

These are your reasons for taking control of your finances and trying to respect this resource. You want your income to go as far as possible in support of living your dreams and following your purpose.

Now it's time for you to come up with your own association with money. Are you fearful that there's never going to be enough and are you saving every dollar you make for a rainy day? Or do you expect there will always be another dollar to be made? You should probably be aiming for somewhere in the middle, and where that point lies is up to you.

Always try to be present when spending money. Be aware of what you're buying and how much it's costing you. Work out how long you have to work to make the money you're spending. And don't get swept away by sales and discounts.

What are your long-term financial goals? For many people, this means buying a house and paying off the mortgage, then investing their money and becoming a self-funded retiree before the age of sixty-five.

When thinking about your long-term financial goals, it's important to consider the lifestyle you want now, and during retirement. Too many people spend beyond their means and never save enough for the future. Saving and investing early in your working life means your investment returns can be partially reinvested and used to supplement your lifestyle.

Take some time to consider your own financial goals, starting with the following questions:

- When do you want to retire?
- Where do you want your children to go to school?
- How much emergency money do you want to have?
- What sort of cars do you want to drive?
- What sort of house do you want to live in/own/rent?
- Where do you want to go on holiday?

Let's consider a race to wealth between Tim and Tom over the course of forty years.

Tim followed the advice in this book and invested $5000 from his first year's income. He saved $5000 each year for ten years and then stopped investing, letting compound interest (reinvesting) do the work for the next thirty years.

Tom, on the other hand, did his own thing for the first five years. He partied, bought flash toys, and generally avoided saving. After five years, he got his life together and started saving $5000 a year, which he did for the next thirty-five years.

Can you guess who ended up with more money at the end of the 40-year period? Keep in mind that Tim invested a total of $50,000 and Tom invested $180,000. Take a look at the following tables.

These tables are based on 10-percent return per annum. The Australian Stock Market equities have an average of 5.9-percent dividend return and 4.2-percent growth = 10.1 percent, including franking credits.

TIM

AGE	INVEST	TOTAL	RETURNS
22	$5,000	$5,000	$500
23	$5,000	$10,500	$1,050
24	$5,000	$16,550	$1,655
25	$5,000	$23,205	$2,321
26	$5,000	$30,526	$3,053
27	$5,000	$38,578	$3,858
28	$5,000	$47,436	$4,744
29	$5,000	$57,179	$5,718
30	$5,000	$67,897	$6,790
31	$5,000	$79,687	$7,969
32		$87,656	$8,766
33		$96,421	$9,642
34		$106,064	$10,606
35		$116,670	$11,667
58		$1,044,698	$104,470
59		$1,149,167	$114,917
60		$1,264,084	$126,408
61		$1,390,493	$139,049
62		$1,529,542	$152,954
Total	$50,000	$1,529,542	$152,954

	TOM		
AGE	INVEST	TOTAL	RETURNS
22			
23			
24			
25			
26			
27	$5,000	$5,000	$500
28	$5,000	$10,500	$1,050
29	$5,000	$16,550	$1,655
30	$5,000	$23,205	$2,321
31	$5,000	$30,526	$3,053
32	$5,000	$38,578	$3,858
33	$5,000	$47,436	$4,744
34	$5,000	$57,179	$5,718
35	$5,000	$67,897	$6,790
58	$5,000	$1,005,689	$100,569
59	$5,000	$1,111,258	$111,126
60	$5,000	$1,227,383	$122,738
61	$5,000	$1,355,122	$135,512
62	$5,000	$1,495,634	$149,563
Total	**$180,000**	**$1,495,634**	**$149,563**

It's easy to understand why Tim absolutely smashed it and came out way ahead of Tom. Not only does compounding interest work, but saving in the early years also sets valuable boundaries around spending habits. It's all too easy to increase spending as your salary increases.

'Compound interest is the eighth wonder of the world. He who understands it, earns it ... he who doesn't ... pays it.'
—ALBERT EINSTEIN.

I thoroughly recommend you read *The Barefoot Investor* by Scott Pape, who is a master at simplifying personal finances. After selling over 1.6 million copies of his book, Pape is leading a movement of financially literate individuals looking to take control of their finances.

If you're not yet convinced of the power of compounding, here is another example.

Take a standard 64-square chessboard. Imagine placing one grain of rice on the first square, then doubling it on each subsequent square as you move across the board. You would have 1, 2, 4, 8, 16, 32, 64, 128 grains of rice at the end of the first row.

By the time you'd finished the entire board and reached the sixty-fourth square, the number would have ballooned to 9,223,372,036,854,780,000 (9 quintillion, 223 quadrillion, 372 trillion, 36 billion, 854 million and 780 thousand) grains of rice.

Sure, you might not be able to double your net worth each year, but as the Tim and Tom example above shows, you can double it every ten years. If you start now, your exponential growth will add up over a 40-year career.

As a final word on finances, take a look into the FIRE (financially independent retire early) movement and have a think about whether it's right for you. This is a popular movement in the Millennial and Gen Z generations, who are looking to retire from work early to live life on their terms. It has totally worked for me, and I truly believe it can work for you, too, if that's what you want.

List your top ten financial goals and roughly what age you want to be when you achieve them:

	FINANCIAL GOALS	**AGE**
1		
2		
3		
4		
5		
6		
7		
8		
9		
10		

CHAPTER 3

Sticky-Note Planner

Now that you have completed your personal pillars you can start planning your future. This can be a massive undertaking; so massive that many never attempt it. However, developing a simple plan really isn't all that hard or scary, and it can be made much easier by using my sticky-note planner.

The best way of using my sticky-note planner is to divide up a whiteboard or A3 sheet of paper into rows and columns as shown below:

- Create a column for each of the decades ahead of your current age: 30's, 40's, 50's, 60's.
- Create a row for each of your four pillars.
- Put the top ten items from each of your pillars (bucket list, career, personal and finances) onto sticky notes and attach

them to your planner, roughly correlating with the age you want to be when you achieve them.

Getting started is the hard part. Get out everything you need (sheets of paper, sticky notes and pens). Take a moment to eliminate distractions, like turning your phone to airplane mode. Now take a moment to do a quick meditation and clear your mind.

Get your whiteboard or sheet of paper ready, take a single sticky note and pen, and start somewhere. Anywhere, it doesn't matter where. Just start. Copy an idea you like from my examples if that makes it easier.

Starting with your bucket list is often a great way to get things moving. Make sure you put down all your bucket-list items on the page. After all, what's the point of having a bucket list if you don't intend to tick off the items on it?

It might help if you use one or two words that will give you a prompt. You could also try using different colours, or putting a red star next to the important items. Remember that sticky notes are removable, so if you don't like where one note is, peel it off and shift it. And if you change your mind about a particular note, scrunch it up and start again.

Once you have a few sticky notes down, start to think about which areas you need to expand on, and try to get the creative juices flowing in that direction until you have a good spread across the board. Move beyond the initial ten ideas from each pillar. Are there any ideas you've missed?

Keep going until you run out of ideas. Feel free to double stack, and write as big or as small as you want. It's your plan, so it's your rules. Continue building your planner until you run out of ideas. When it becomes a struggle, stop. You can always come back and add more sticky notes down the track.

	20's	30's	40's	50's	60's
BUCKET LIST	SKYDIVING	INDOOR ROCK CLIMB	PYRAMIDS / TOP GUN FLIGHT		
CAREER	GRADUATE		GENERAL MANAGER / START OWN BUSINESS	RETIRE	
PERSONAL	GET ESTABLISHED	MARRIED / KIDS *2	BUY A BOAT		
FINANCES	START INVESTING	HOUSE SAVINGS / BUY HOUSE	PAY OFF HOUSE	$3M INVESTED	

CHAPTER 3: STICKY-NOTE PLANNER | 67

Once you've exhausted your brain and your stack of sticky notes, stand back for a bit of reflection. Now it's time to shuffle things around if you need to. Ask yourself if there are any decades that you have put way too many activities into. If so, now is the time to decide what needs to come forward or to be pushed back.

Have you included anything overly ambitious that would require a little more time to achieve? Have you left something too late in life? (If you have indoor rock-climbing on your bucket list, it might not pay to wait until you're sixty to try it.) Are any sticky notes no longer relevant? Have you doubled up on some that can be removed? Are there any notes that would be better moved to another location?

Now it's time to pad things out a bit, and expand on each of the sticky notes in a little more detail. You can either write in your notebook or type out this information. For each sticky note, write out a detailed paragraph explaining the ins and outs of the item listed. Try to structure your plan in a way that makes sense to you. There are two ways of doing this:

1. Start with your categories and break them down into ten-year brackets.

Table A showing categories

PERSONAL LIFE	20's	30's	40's	50's	60's
CAREER	20's	30's	40's	50's	60's
FINANCE	20's	30's	40's	50's	60's
BUCKET LIST	20's	30's	40's	50's	60's

2. Start with ten-year brackets and break them down into categories.

Table B showing ten-year brackets

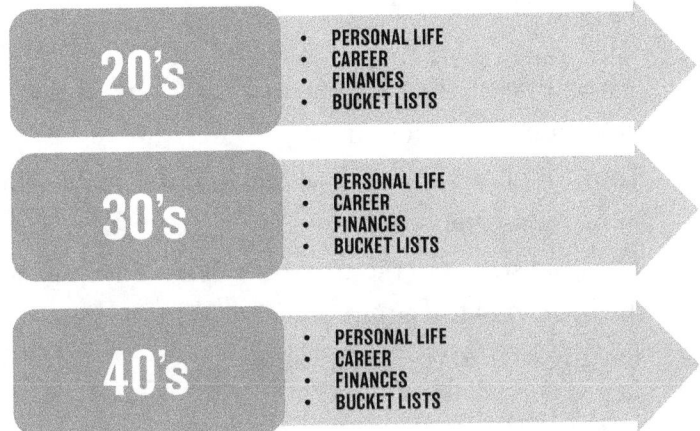

Congratulations, you have your very own future planner.

Visualising a goal coming to fruition is one of the most powerful forms of motivation, and it can be used in everyday life. For instance, if you plan on running a charity race, picture yourself crossing the finish line, right down to feeling the emotions you would expect to experience. This vision is your motivation. If you believe it, and feel it strongly enough, you have all the motivation you need.

'If you can dream it you can do it.'

—WALT DISNEY

Some key points to visualising goals successfully:

- Generate a crystal-clear image of your goal. How does it look, smell and feel?
- What emotions will you feel when you've achieved your goal?
- When you're crystal clear on what your goal is, devise a timeframe to achieve it.
- Think about what you're willing to invest to make it a reality (time, effort, money).
- The final step is to picture yourself already in possession of the goal. Feel the emotions of the achievement; you're now starting to find your motivation.

'Visualisation works if you work hard. That's the thing. You can't just visualise and go eat a sandwich.'

—JIM CARREY

If you only do one practical exercise from this entire book, make sure it's the sticky-note planner. Not only will you create an exciting picture of your future, but you'll also have a powerful planning tool you can use for many aspects of your life and career.

Download the full sticky-note planner tool here: (https://rapidmentoring.com.au/bookresources/).

Use this QR code to access the Rapid sticky-note planner.

CHAPTER 4

Discovering Your Purpose

Finding purpose and passion in life is a significant breakthrough for anyone. Some people are lucky enough to have gained a deep-seated understanding at a young age of why they were put on Earth. Others, like me, take longer to find their true calling in life.

My journey to finding purpose started when I found myself getting increasingly agitated in my career. I knew there had to be something else in my life, something that would bring me joy rather than stress me out. So I started recording the top five things I was grateful for at the end of each day. Mentoring and coaching the younger team members often found its way onto my list. It took a good twelve months from the day I started to clearly define my personal *why*.

Perhaps start your journey with a book. A favourite of mine is *Purpose* by Lisa Messenger. This was one of the first personal-development books I read, and it was a massive help on my journey. I also recommend you read *Start with Why* by Simon Sinek. It's one of the most popular self-help books for good reason.

Finding purpose in life really does get a bad rap. Many people see this topic as overly spiritual, where you need to go away on a hippy retreat to a secluded beach and meditate for twenty hours per day so the universe can bring you a clear mental picture of your life's purpose. It doesn't need to be this way, although I think it would be kind of cool to go on a 20-hour meditation retreat, but each to their own. Sadly, vast proportions of the population never explore this concept or are not even vaguely aware of it.

So it's important that you find what you're passionate about, then make this your work or, at the very least, allow work to fulfil your passions in other ways.

Your purpose in life has a whole lot to do with your four pillars. You can also add to this mix your personality, values and strengths. You're always going to work harder on the things you enjoy and that you're strongest at. For instance, it would be hard to believe your purpose is to be a keynote speaker if you vomit prior to going on stage.

Your personal strengths are an interesting insight into your purpose. Many might say that we all need to focus on developing our weaknesses. While in some circumstances I do agree that you need to develop your weaknesses to an acceptable level, I strongly recommend that you focus on developing your strengths even further. Developing your weaknesses will make you average, but developing your strengths will make you extraordinary.

So many people I have worked with over the past fifteen years have constantly complained that they did not know what they wanted to do with their life. The sad part is that many of these people were approaching retirement age with a limited time left to find their purpose. Other younger members of my teams were just willing to bob around at sea and see what life brought.

Often the biggest hurdle to gaining this level of self-awareness is actually having the courage to acknowledge to ourselves what we want to achieve. Sure, we all have hopes and dreams. It's another thing to write them down, define our purpose, and put an action plan in place to really get living.

After reading and working through the four pillars in earlier chapters, focusing on your strengths and working through the exercises, you should now have more clarity around your life purpose. I encourage you to continue your journey of discovery. When you have an unwavering conviction about what that purpose is, your life will take on new meaning.

To close this chapter, I want you to think about what your personal legacy will be. When your days are done, how will you be remembered? What will people say in your obituary? Even if your funeral is a long way off (and I hope it is), spend some time writing down a few thoughts about what you would want people to say about you. Would a dramatic shift be required to get you there from where you currently are? Do you have wild aspirations that you need to get after right away?

On a blank notebook page, jot down some ideas of how you want to be remembered, the person you want to become. This can be as short or as long as you like, but as usual I do recommend that you write this down. You can destroy it afterwards if you like. This is not an exercise in caring what others think; it's about how you want to be remembered.

Remember, the only way you can control time is to choose when you will act. You only get 86,400 seconds in a day and you only get to use those seconds once, so make the most of them. If you want to become a billionaire by the age of sixty, the easiest path is to start building towards that goal *today*. There will never be a better time.

CHAPTER 5

Phased Attention

At this stage of the book, you will have taken stock of your four personal pillars and completed the sticky-note planner. Now it's time to apply some phases of detailed attention. Self-awareness is a great place to start. By working through some of these examples you will really start to master where you're heading in life.

Using your sticky-note planner, take as long as you need to brainstorm everything you want to achieve in your life, and categorise these things under the four pillars. Your career goals might look something like this:

- Achieve the level of general manager
- Start my own business
- Become a keynote speaker
- Write a book

- Run a podcast
- Write blogs
- Manage a team

When contemplating the decade ahead, what can you start working towards right now? Decide on a maximum of one or two items. Once you have mastered these items, what would you work on next? The whole point here is to generate phases of focused attention. You don't want to be overwhelmed trying to write blogs while learning how to be a public speaker while writing a book while trying to launch a new business. Pick one or two things that you can focus on now. For example:

- Year one: write a blog
- Year two: learn public speaking
- Year three: run a podcast and write a book

Not everything has to happen at once. Fulfilling your ultimate goal is all about building up the blocks gradually so you can get where you want to be. It won't happen overnight, but it will happen.

* * *

So far, we've covered a great deal of practical and useful content and exercises, with the specific intention of helping you find direction in your life. We started with the fundamentals—your personality and values, and how they shape who you are as person. We looked at some of the tricks played by mindset, and as a result you now know that you're enough. We've also discussed your personal pillars—where you want your career to take you and what your ideal personal life looks like.

To pull it all together, you have been introduced to the sticky-note planner, a powerful tool to help you comprehensively map out your desired future. Hopefully you now have a better picture of where you're heading and the potential routes you can take to get there. With a destination in mind, it's now time to plan for the journey ahead.

PART 2
PACK YOUR BAGS

CHAPTER 6

Preparation

In preparing for the journey ahead, you need to equip yourself with the tools you require to get the job done. That means getting the job done under any circumstance, regardless of what is thrown your way. There are very few certainties ahead in any career, and even when there are, some can be quite negative. Regardless of what career you choose, you will undoubtedly be placed in stressful situations from time to time; expected to deal with difficult people; stretched beyond your comfort zone; or simply offered opportunities you think are outside your reach.

This section is focused on establishing a framework that will allow you to release any career pressure and make sure you feel like you're in control. Remember, *you* are holding the map and regulating how fast or slow things move. As the Boy Scouts always say, 'Be prepared!'

Let's start building your survival kit, and putting steps in place to shift those difficult parts of your life to autopilot so you never need to stress about them.

Before you start, congratulations on all the work you've done so far on mapping out your personal pillars. This work will come in very handy in the following pages.

MOTIVATION

What are your motivators in life? Motivation is a key factor that determines whether people will decide to do an activity; how long they are willing to sustain the activity; and how hard they are going to work at pursuing the activity.

Your motivation will often be closely aligned to your highest values. After all, it's very hard to get motivated about something you don't value. For example, you would find it very hard to be motivated to run a marathon if fitness wasn't one of your top values.

Motivation can be either extrinsic or intrinsic.

Extrinsic motivation is when you're driven by external reward such as money, treats, fame or accolades.

Intrinsic motivation is when the impetus comes from within, when you're driven by internal reward. You do things because they please you and make you feel good, generally because they're aligned with fulfilling your values.

Intrinsic motivation is by far the most powerful; you do things because you want to, not because someone else wants you to. When you want to find motivation to do something, identify why it will make you feel good, and why it will help you fulfil your values. Finding these intrinsic motivators will help you light a spark, and stay inspired and on task—and will be much more powerful than doing things to please others.

Now you are ready to link goals to motivation. For example, if you've had a lifetime dream of going indoor rock-climbing but feel that you're way too unfit to give it a try, now is the time to visualise the goal and turn that visualisation into motivation. Picture yourself harnessed up in your finest rock-climbing gear. The chalk is on your fingers and you start to ascend the wall. You grip the holds with your fingers and push upwards with your legs. You're doing it! Feel the excitement, the adrenaline, the nervous trepidation. This is your visualisation, your motivation.

You will feel your motivation dwindle when you have to make yourself do something you don't necessarily want or need to do. It could be work for other people, or work you don't really care about. In these instances, you need to start looking at the bigger picture, aiming for the point where you can frame a visualisation that brings positive results for you.

While you may not want to work on a particular task, achieving it with a noteworthy outcome could do wonders for your reputation. By finding ways to align a task with your values, you will find intrinsic rather than extrinsic motivation, and complete it happily and well. Conversely, adopting a negative attitude and doing a bad job will leave your reputation in tatters.

In the first part of this book, you saw why planning your journey is so important. You need to have a greater career goal. You must always be motivated to strive for that next level.

If you're struggling to get motivated about your job, you know it's time to revisit your values. In the next exercises, try listing your top five values and linking them to your job:

MY TOP VALUES

1.
2.
3.
4.
5.

Now try listing twenty ways that your job helps you fulfil your values. If you can do this, your motivation will come back:

WAYS THAT MY JOB HELPS ME LIVE MY VALUES

1.
2.
3.
4.
5.
6.
7.
8.
9.
10.
11.
12.
13.

14	
15	
16	
17	
18	
19	
20	

There are two books about motivation that I highly recommend you read. *The Motivation Manifesto* by Brendon Burchard will turn you from a household kitten into a raging tiger, and *The 10X Rule* by Grant Cardone will challenge you to think ten times bigger and try ten times harder. Both these books will help you find your motivation and face your fears.

FEARS

What are your fears? No, I'm not talking about being scared of spiders or heights. Think about more personal fears. Do you have any fears that are holding you back, or that will hold you back in the future? These are some of the most common fears that prevent people from reaching their full potential:

- Public speaking
- Networking/socialising
- Failure
- Success
- What other people will think
- Personal perception
- Disappointing someone they care about

I'm sure you can add to this list with your own fears. To overcome your fears you need to step outside your safe areas. As many people before me have said, great things happen on the other side of your comfort zone. Try to consider your future and how your fears will impact your results. For instance, if you want to become CEO of the company, chances are high that you will need to speak in front of large crowds. If you're afraid of public speaking, you will need to overcome this fear.

Look at each of the fears you have identified that hold you back, and think about how you can start breaking them down. Look at them from a different angle and reframe them, if you can.

Let's look again at our example of public speaking, a very common fear for many people. (I have definitely had this fear. Even though I've never had a bad experience, I have always hated the thought of speaking in front of a crowd.)

A first step would be to change your internal language. Instead of saying *I hate public speaking*, change it to something softer that stops the negative reinforcement you keep giving yourself. Try to use wording like *I'm not good at public speaking yet.* The *yet* at the end of the sentence is vitally important. It tells the brain that you are going to become good at public speaking, it is achievable, and your current state is not set in concrete.

You could start by speaking to a small group of people or a large group of children; both groups are probably less intimidating than a large group of adults. You might fear that people will think less of you because of what you say, but consider the possibility that they might think *more* of you.

One way to look into fears is to start at a high level and start breaking things down. Sure, you might be afraid of public speaking, but why?

It's important to dig down into these fears and assess the root cause. You might be fearful of what one person in the audience thinks, even anticipating the possibility that they will confront you over it, but consider the flip side. It's equally possible that they will come up and congratulate you for your presentation.

Find the root fear and try to reframe it.

The five-*why* process is a powerful investigative method, a technique developed in the 1930s by Sakichi Toyoda, the founder of Toyota Industries. The technique is still widely used and taught today through the Six Sigma project-management system. To use the technique, you simply keep diving deeper with each *why* question you ask. The purpose of the five-*why* process is to get to the root cause of the issue, and create a countermeasure to ensure the problem does not repeat itself.

As an example, let's say that one day you're late to work because your trusty Toyota let you down:

1. Why did the car break down? *This question might reveal that your car had a flat tyre.*
2. Why did it have a flat tyre? *This question might reveal that there was a small nail in the tyre and the spare tyre was flat also.*
3. Why was there a nail in the tyre? *This question might reveal that your tyres are worn down.*
4. Why were the tyres worn right down and the spare flat? *This question might reveal a lack of maintenance.*
5. Why the tyres were poorly maintained? *This question might reveal that the car hadn't had its scheduled service.*

From this point on, you can establish that if you implement a regular service regime (replacing the worn tyres and repairing the spare) you should be able to prevent this situation from occurring again. Another effective approach to overcoming your fears is to try a neurolinguistic programming (NLP) reframing exercise.

1. In your notebook, open a page and head it up 'My current beliefs about public speaking'. List the first five words you would use to describe your feelings about public speaking.

You might choose words like *intimidated, anxious, gut-wrenching, nauseating, blank mind*. Yes, they are all negative, which means you would be more likely to fear public speaking and become nervous whenever you face it, which would not help your performance on stage.

	MY CURRENT BELIEFS ABOUT PUBLIC SPEAKING
1	
2	
3	
4	
5	

Let's see how you can reframe this negative bias towards public speaking. Keep in mind that the right amount of stress can produce adrenaline, help you focus on the task at hand, and actually drive optimal performance. Ultimately, you want to be able to look at the task at hand as a challenge, not a problem. Reframing is all about trying to see the opposite side to a problem. If you see the negatives, try to look for the positives. Rather than seeing the bad that could come from a situation, seek the good that could come from it.

2. Head up another page 'My new beliefs about public speaking'. Examples could include *spreading my message, connecting with the audience, increasing my personal brand, enjoyable.*

MY NEW BELIEFS ABOUT PUBLIC SPEAKING	
1	
2	
3	
4	
5	

Public speaking is a particularly good example to address. Here is a wry quote from Jerry Seinfeld: 'According to most studies, people's number one fear is public speaking. Number two is death. Death is number two. Does that sound right? This means to the average person, if you go to a funeral, you're better off in the casket than doing the eulogy.'

Another astute description of the fear of public speaking comes from Scott Berkun, author of *Confessions of a Public Speaker*: 'Any time you're an animal standing alone on an open plain, with no weapon or anywhere to hide and dozens if not thousands of eyeballs trained on you, evolutionarily speaking, you're about to die!'

Perhaps this helps explain this innate fear that many people have of standing on stage.

This reframing activity can be used for almost every aspect of your life. Do you hate going to the gym? If the words you associate with the word *gym* include *pain, hard work, anxiousness, soreness, stress*, perhaps you would feel a lot better about going there if you replaced them with *endorphins, fun, healthy, challenge, goals, attractive*.

A fear of failure is another common concern that people have. Fear of failure is natural, and most of us have to deal with it at some point in time. This fear is a way for our brains to attempt to keep us safe, to prevent us from hurting ourselves.

A fear of failure, however, can also cripple your creativity, crush your dreams and lead to a safe, boring life where you never reach your fullest potential.

While you can use this same reframing exercise for dealing with a fear of failure, I also encourage you to explore past failures. What did you learn from these past failures? What benefits came from them?

I realise it can be difficult to put a positive spin on a past failure, but it really will help your mindset moving forward if you can do it. When you reach the point where you can be grateful for the experience, you're well on your way to crushing your fear of failure. Failure is an inevitable part of life. Go easy on yourself when you do fail, and always look for the lessons you can be grateful for.

Once you have identified your fears, I recommend that you lean in and step towards the fear. If you have a fear of being on video, find a secluded place and record yourself talking. Watch the video and note the things you're not happy with. Re-record the same video and try to incorporate any changes or ideas you noted from your playback.

'Inaction breeds doubt and fear. Action breeds confidence and courage. If you want to conquer fear, do not sit home and think about it. Go out and get busy.'
—DALE CARNEGIE

Continual exposure to your fears is one of the most effective ways to overcome them. Picture yourself sitting with the thing you fear, be okay with it in the room, and try to relax in its presence. Over time you will become more and more comfortable.

Start small and build your way up. Stepping outside your comfort zone isn't easy, but it's rewarding.

CHAPTER 7

Confidence

Have you ever noticed how your beliefs can impact your ability to achieve goals? As infants we have an innate, unwavering belief system. We believe that no matter how many times we fail, one day we will master the task. Yet later on in life we often find ourselves lacking the confidence to try anything for the first time because we're afraid of failure.

Imagine yourself, at your current age, learning to walk. After falling down a few times, can you picture yourself saying, 'No, this isn't for me. I think I'll crawl.'

Now imagine your ability to succeed in life if your mindset was always: *I can do this. I just need to have the right mindset. Things might not be perfect, but I'll give it my best shot. I'll try my best to achieve it.*

Next time you find an obstacle in your path, run at it with confidence, tackle it head on. You might be surprised at how much easier it is for you to overcome obstacles if you take them on with confidence. When you fail, and you will, remember to keep the same unwavering confidence: the belief that you can overcome any setback.

Over the years I've read my fair share of the fake-it-till-you-make-it strategies. I don't like them at all. People can tell when you're faking it, and it just isn't a good look. Consider this: if you can stand up on a stage in front of a crowd and fake it, why on earth can't you stand up in front of a crowd when you're being authentic and genuine?

This whole notion of faking it really grates on me. If you need to do something, know *why* you need to do it. Determine how it helps you fulfil your values. Look for the positives. Muster up the courage and do it.

You could end up damaging your personal brand if you fake your way through life. Yes, faking it definitely does impact your personal brand—it's easy to tell if someone is putting on a front when you read their CV or LinkedIn profile.

Confidence breeds confidence. The more you achieve by facing your fears, the more confident you will become. This will lead to you having an even greater belief in your own abilities. No, acting confident and facing your fears are not faking it; that's called *believing in your own abilities*. There is a massive difference.

CHAPTER 8

Strengths

Personal development is generally broken down into two areas of growth: strengths and weaknesses. Be careful when it comes to focusing all your efforts on improving your weaknesses or perceived 'development areas'. This might sound counterintuitive, but I am a firm believer that we excel in and enjoy the things that we are good at. By all means improve your development areas until they are at a competent level, but since these can often be areas that offer you little excitement or reward, why spend your time improving them when you could be improving your strengths? Would a right-handed bowler learn how to bowl left-handed just in case? No.

Throughout my university years I struggled with computer programming. I wasn't good at it and didn't enjoy it, and I barely scraped through my programming subjects. Since then I have never needed to touch a piece of code. It goes to show that you don't have to be good at everything.

Developing natural talents in your strength areas will not only be enjoyable, but you will also reap substantial benefits far beyond being a total all-rounder. Don't forget that as you progress through your career, you can always engage other people to plug your weaknesses, leaving you to focus on your strengths.

As an example, let's assume that you're frustrated with the financial part of your role (i.e. balancing the books). You still need to understand the basics of what you're managing, but you could engage a cost controller or finance manager to take care of it for you, leaving you to focus on what you're good at.

Consider the equation below. It's a very simple multiplier chart that indicates how talent and effort interact. In other words, if we take a talent and multiply it by effort (investment of our time and the heart we put into things), we get a strength value.

$$[TALENT] \times [EFFORT] = [STRENGTH]$$

1. Rate your natural talent in a specific area from 0 to 5 (0 being no talent and 5 being extremely naturally talented).
2. Now multiply this score by the amount of effort you're willing to put into it (0 you don't enjoy it or want to spend time on it versus 5 if you absolutely love it and want to make it your life's work).

For example, if you take something you're not talented at and don't enjoy doing, you might score your natural talent as a 2 and the effort you're willing to put into learning this new skill as a 1. The result would be a strength of 2.

For a left-field example, consider two basketball players:

- Jim is 185 centimetres (6'1) tall and naturally athletic (talent is a 5). He enjoys basketball and likes to play socially. He trains twice a week, but it's not his life work (say a 3 for effort).

    5 [TALENT] x 3 [EFFORT] = 15 [STRENGTH]

- Bobby, on the other hand, is only 155 centimetres (5'1) tall and unfit (talent of 2, being generous). He wants to make it into the big league and trains four times a week, devoting as much time to it as possible (effort of 4).

    2 [TALENT] x 4 [EFFORT] = 8 [STRENGTH]

It's easy to see how Jim would easily outperform Bobby in a one-on-one game.

Finally, consider if Jim had Bobby's dedication to basketball. The equation would now look like this:

5 [TALENT] x 4 [EFFORT] = 20 [STRENGTH]

When it comes to building a team, you want to ensure that it's as strong as possible. It's important to always recruit your team around your personal strengths and weaknesses, and the strengths and weaknesses of the rest of the team. There's no reason to have a team of people with exactly the same skillsets unless you need them to replicate a particular task. Try not to have others replicating your work. Often they won't do things exactly how you want and you'll just get frustrated because you didn't do it yourself.

I always prefer to build my team with people who are talented in areas that I am not, or who will do the work I don't want to do. Knowing my strengths and weaknesses means that I can structure a team around them.

These concepts are derived from Tom Rath's book, *Strengths Finder 2.0*. This book is an instructive read; however, the true benefit comes from the online personality-profile test. I recommend that you get yourself a copy of *Strengths Finder 2.0* and work through the exercises. Once you know your talent or strength areas, you can read up on the appropriate areas within the book and learn how to expand and capitalise on them.

Ultimately, being perfectly rounded will make you average. Focusing and applying your time to your natural talents, however, will make you exceptional in certain areas. This result will encourage you to take the lead in your strength areas, making these the focus of whatever you do in your chosen career.

Consider the 'natural' salesman. Does it make sense to keep that person in the office balancing the books when they're not good at maths? Or should they be in the showroom doing what they do best and enjoy the most, which is selling?

My absolute recommendation is that you discover your own personal strengths and develop these into your superpowers. Knowing your strengths and weaknesses will allow you to avoid the things you're not good at, leaving you free to focus your time and effort on the areas you actually excel at.

CHAPTER 8

Mental Strength

As you're probably aware, the human mind is capable of an amazing array of emotions. Most of us have, at some time in our lives, experienced the deepest sadness as well as the most exhilarating joy and laughter. Many of us are not aware though that we actually have the power to change how we are feeling. Yes, we can be in control of our emotions. Simply being aware of our emotional state can allow us to objectively view how we are currently feeling, and make a conscious decision to change our state.

It almost becomes an action plan. If you can identify that you are down and you don't want to be, you can choose to do things to boost your mood. You need to come up with your own list of things that can help in this regard. It could be as simple as listening to happier music, or as complicated as removing yourself from a situation that is bringing you down.

Look at the following chart that lists a range of emotions and rates them from 0–100, where 0 is absolutely depressed and 100 is euphorically ecstatic (the happiest you could ever imagine yourself).

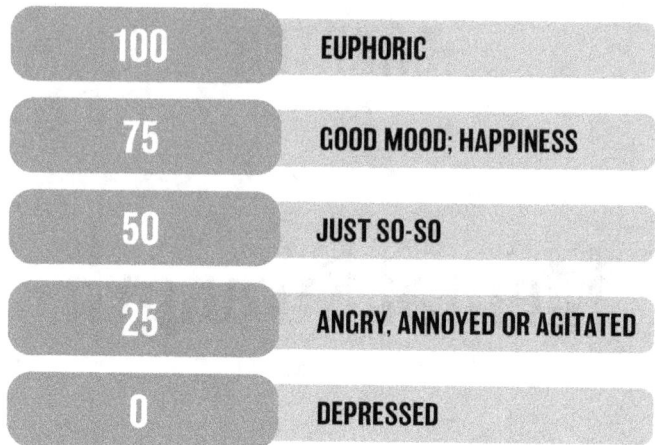

Now bring out your inner scientist and try a little experiment:

- Measure your current emotional state on a scale of 0–100, using the above chart.
- Listen to a minute of 'Dancing on My Own' by Calum Scott. How does this song shift your emotional state?
- Now listen to Pharrell Williams' song 'Because I Am Happy'. Get up and dance around for a minute or two. Or try 'I Gotta Feeling' by the Black Eyed Peas, or 'Hey Ya!' by OutKast (you can make your own happy playlist).
- How do these actions shift your emotional state?
- Did you notice a shift in your emotional state purely from the music you listened to?

I'm not suggesting that you should always listen to upbeat, happy music. What you listen to prior to or during a massage can impact your level of relaxation. Similarly, what you listen to before a sporting event can pump you up and improve your performance.

This exercise offers a tangible example of how you can control your emotional state, even if it's just a small shift. You're in control. If you ever find yourself becoming emotional, sit back, reflect on how you're feeling, and look for ways to elevate your mood.

There is a lot of information available on this topic. I recommend *The Map of Human Emotional Consciousness* by David R Hawkins, or check out some of the videos on emotions by Tony Robbins.

Keep in mind that it's perfectly okay to experience a range of human emotions. If you're experiencing loss, it's okay to grieve. But having an awareness of the tools at your disposal means you can bring yourself out of this state when you decide the time is right.

It's a similar scenario with anger. If something has upset you and you're angry, it's okay to feel this way and to take the time to process things. You might listen to some angry music, or go for a run to get it out of your system. Then you need to make the conscious decision to bring yourself out of the angry state, once you feel you have sufficiently expressed this feeling.

Feelings of anger could be sending you a message. It's important to identify why you feel this way. There might be times when you consciously want to move from being happy and joyful to energised, for example getting pumped up for a gym session or a football match. In the latter example, it's important that you bring your mood back up with a few beers with the team and have a laugh when the game is over.

This will highlight how capable you are of moving yourself into different zones, depending on the situation. With practice, you should be able to harness this skill to your advantage.

RECHARGE YOUR BATTERIES

If you think of your general wellbeing as a battery, when you are tired, rundown, stressed and sick you could think of it as your battery being depleted to the point that you are running on empty. If you maintain an awareness of your battery levels, you can more actively monitor and maintain those levels.

If you notice your batteries are becoming low, you need to look for ways to recharge them. You could do this by taking time out for yourself, relaxing, spending time with friends, or whatever you enjoy doing.

Holidays and annual leave will help you to recharge, as will planning a holiday, which ensures that you have something to look forward to in the future. Holidays don't need to be expensive or extravagant, you just need to ensure that you get value from your time off. Dedicating some time to recharging your batteries is the key. Remember that introverts and extraverts will recharge in different ways.

Here's a challenge for you: What are your battery levels like right now? Try to give yourself a percentage figure, much like charging a device; it can really help to put a number on it.

Similar to how much charge your phone has, you need to come up with the same analogy for your own batteries. You need to be aware when you're starting to run low so you can take the time to recharge.

It's also important to recharge during the workday. Many busy people think they are being more productive by working through their lunchbreak, when in fact the opposite is true. Giving yourself a break to recharge your batteries throughout the day means you will actually be far more productive when you return to work. Even a 5–10-minute break away from the desk can do wonders for recharging batteries.

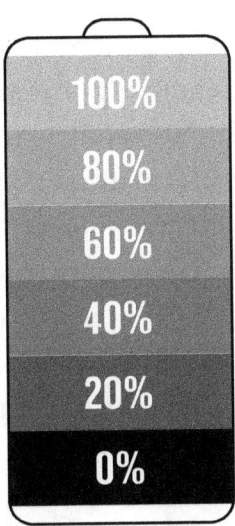

Now it's time to find something to charge things up a bit. Here is a great example of how easily you can take a reset at any point in your day. Focus on your breathing, notice the breath coming in and out your nose or mouth, feel your lungs expand and contract. Now follow these steps:

1. Breathe in for a count of 1, 2, 3, 4 and feel the pause at the top.
2. Exhale for a count of 1, 2, 3, 4, 5, 6, 7 and feel the pause at the bottom.
3. Repeat this at least five times. Congratulations, you've just performed a super-simple, quick brain reset.

GRATITUDE

I am a solid believer in the power of gratitude. Gratitude begins with acknowledging what you are thankful for, and will help to boost your mindset and think more positively. Adding a gratitude activity to your daily routine is scientifically proven to improve physical and psychological health. Gratitude can help to boost your mood, make you more thankful for the life you live, and help you become a whole lot happier. It can also increase mental strength, reduce anxiety, reduce aggression, help you sleep better at night, and improve your self-esteem.

Trust me, it works. Do it at least once a day. Ask yourself each night what three things you can be grateful for that day. The more things you can list the better, and the more times a day you repeat the task the better.

One way you can take your gratitude to the next level is to show others your appreciation. Thank someone when they're not expecting it. Write a positive review for someone when they've done a good job. Buy a small gift to say 'thank you'. Doing these things will not only increase your gratitude and give your personal life a boost, but will also give other people a massive boost too.

Spread the love; make the world a better place.

CHAPTER 10

Stress

Stress is an inherent part of everyday life. Some people are naturally able to deal with it quite well, while others cope poorly. In some ways we actually need a little stress in our lives. An achievable deadline or another kind of pressure can help to get the adrenaline flowing, allowing us to perform at our peak.

The main issue I see surrounding stress (excluding the negative impact it can have on the mind and body) is expectation. Many people are subjected to extensive amounts of stress, and are expected to deal with it without being taught what it actually is or how to cope with it.

Stress is caused by a perceived imbalance between the things you have to do and the resources that you have available to complete those tasks. If you believe that the tasks you have to do outweigh the resources or time you have available, this will cause you stress.

Stress can also be seen as a type of fear. For instance, you might experience fear that you can't get something done on time, or will disappoint someone, or won't be good enough. The list goes on.

Interestingly, not everyone becomes stressed over the same things. This is because everyone has their own individual drivers, experiences and triggers that contribute to the stress they feel in different situations. Stress is not inevitable. You *choose* to respond to a situation by becoming stressed. The healthier option would be to identify your triggers, become aware of when you might be triggered, and put strategies in place to address them.

Consider a situation where you have been triggered in the past, and think about the many different ways that you could have handled the situation. At one end of the spectrum you panic and start pulling your hair out; at the other end you calmly state, 'I've got this'. Whenever you find yourself in a stressful situation it's always good to take a calm approach and ask yourself how you can best handle the situation. How you choose to deal with the situation is exactly that: a *choice*.

Stress occurs when you feel out of control and don't know what to do. The antidote to feeling out of control is to take back that control. You can accomplish this by focusing on what you *can* do, and by putting a strategy in place to assist with the challenges you're facing:

1. Firstly, ask yourself how stressed you are. Give your stress a rating out of 10.
2. Now write down all the things that are stressing you right now.
3. Finally, create a list of things you can do to alleviate the stress by eliminating the causes. This list of stress-alleviating items should include positive, proactive and healthy choices.

The idea here is establish healthy coping mechanisms. For instance, if you're feeling tense and pent up because a deadline is looming, getting up from your chair and moving around or exercising for five minutes can relieve the stress. Moving your body can also help clear your head, allowing you to function at a higher capacity until you complete your task.

Becoming self-aware of your stress levels is taking a huge step in the right direction. Once you can assess the level of stress you're experiencing, you can proactively assess the resources required to complete the task and ensure these resources are available.

Recalling the neurolinguistic programming (NLP) reframing exercise from the chapter on fears, you can apply the same principles for stress:

1. Take a scrap of paper and at the top write 'My current beliefs about stress'. Below this write out the first five words you would use to describe stress.

	MY CURRENT BELIEFS ABOUT STRESS
1	
2	
3	
4	
5	

When I've done this in the past I have come up with words like *tension, overwhelmed, struggle, pressure* and *anxious*. Yes, they are all negative. If your own list consists of negative words it means you are more likely to fear stress and become anxious whenever you face that stress. This won't help you achieve the task at hand.

2. In this second step you can reframe your negative bias towards stress. Again, reframing is all about trying to see the opposite side of a problem. In other words, if you see the negatives, try instead to look for the positives. Rather than seeing the bad that could come from a situation, seek the good that could come from it.

Write out your new heading 'My new beliefs about stress'. Below this, list five new associations with stress. Examples could include: *challenge, focus, motivation, initiative, game time,* which are all positive words.

	MY NEW BELIEFS ABOUT STRESS
1	
2	
3	
4	
5	

Consider the pressure newspaper publishers must face on a daily basis, with looming deadlines, getting the final edit signed off, and making sure the issue is on the printing press on time. Some people would lose their minds, while others actually flourish in this environment, getting a rush from the excitement of meeting those deadlines. It all comes down to mindset.

It's very important to start developing stress-coping mechanisms in times of low stress. These strategies need to become habitual and readily available. By the time you've become stressed, you're too worked up to think about not being stressed, and then you get stressed out because you're so stressed, and it snowballs from there. Trust me, I've been there. It's also worth noting that everything seems to go wrong when you're stressed out.

Learning how to manage your own stress is one of the greatest lessons you will learn. It's crucial you learn to do this early in your career, and continue to refine this skill as your life and career invariably change.

SWITCHING OFF

One aspect of life that eluded me for quite a while was the ability to switch off. I'd often continue to think about work after I'd arrived home, or, even worse, found myself checking emails late in the evening and getting worked up if I read something that should have waited for the next day. This invariably messed with my ability to go to sleep at night. Instead, my brain often considered bedtime the perfect quiet time to process everything and try to solve the problems of my day.

To protect your personal life from outside influences you need to establish some key boundaries. For instance, commit yourself to believing that work doesn't impact your personal life, and vice versa. You'll need to work at creating a routine and developing habits that allow you to switch off from work the instant you step inside your home in the evening.

I'm a firm supporter of doing one thing at a time. If you're at work, be at work and don't let your home life impact your work. If you're at home, be at home, and don't let your work ruin your personal time.

The Rapid-debrief technique is one such tool that can help you switch off from work and create a boundary between your two worlds. On a sheet of paper, write down the following three questions. For twenty-one days straight, set an alarm on your phone for a time just before you leave work, or as soon as you get home in the evening, and list three points below each question:

- What are three things I achieved today?
    1. _____
    2. _____
    3. _____

- What are three things I need to achieve tomorrow?
    1. _____
    2. _____
    3. _____

- What are three things I can be grateful for from today?
    1. _____
    2. _____
    3. _____

Yes, it's that simple. But there are a few ground rules:

- You must write your answers down. Simply thinking about them is not enough. Writing things down is profoundly more powerful than thought alone. Writing them out in a diary is a good way to keep a daily record.
- Allow twenty-one days straight to achieve best results, and do the exercises at the same time every day. Many people

report improvements at around day five, so please keep going until it's become a habit in your daily routine.
- Avoid doing the exercise just before bed because it can make your brain too active and start you thinking about all you need to do the next day.

There is another powerful way of reinforcing this exercise. Before you open the door to enter your home in the evening, ask yourself who you want to be when you walk inside. By doing this, you set the intention of the person you want to be at home.

Switch off your work emails in the evening and safeguard this time as your own. Do you want to be the grumpy workaholic who is totally bent out of shape and exhausted by work? Or do you want to be the loving partner and the fun parent who somehow finds a new lease on life after they arrive home?

Learning to switch off at the end of the day is such a valuable lesson. It will transform your home life and alleviate your stress. It will also help to ensure that you get a decent night's sleep to help you perform at your peak the following day.

SLEEP

Your ability to get a good night's sleep has a powerful impact on your career progression, and your general wellbeing. Sleep is a major part of self-care and the rejuvenation of your body. Over the years I have really struggled with sleep, especially when I've been under immense pressure and stress. If I had slept better at those times, I know I would have performed better. If nothing else, I would have been less stressed, irritable and anxious.

Getting a good night's sleep can have the following benefits:

- Improved concentration and awareness
- Lowered risk of heart disease
- Better athletic performance and recovery
- Prevents depression
- Lower inflammation in the body
- Strengthens the immune system
- Helps to prevent burnout

As you can see, getting a decent night's sleep is very important. Ideally, you should be aiming for seven to eight hours each night.

Being an engineer essentially means I've been trained to solve problems. My problem over the years has been that I used bedtime as the ideal time to process the activities of my day, to think about all the unsolved problems and effectively go into problem-solving mode. My brain would become a whirlpool of different thoughts, all bouncing around hypothesising different outcomes for the issues of the day. I would lie there feeling anxious about not getting enough sleep, then start calculating how much sleep I would get if I nodded off in the next five minutes. And if I didn't fall asleep, I would become even more anxious and restless.

Now, you won't learn much from a person who has never had a sleep issue. Here are some of my personal insights, the things I have learned about getting a better night's sleep, and I'm sure they will help both the best and the worst sleepers.

Even if you're a good sleeper, make sure you read on so you don't undo your good habits. You might even improve your current habits and reduce the risk of stress impacting your sleep down the track. If you struggle to get enough sleep, the solution is simple; refining the solution to suit your needs is where things get tricky.

Firstly, you need to create a new bedtime routine. Sounds simple, right? Wrong. There are literally thousands of go-to-sleep methods out there. Finding the right one for you is where it gets difficult, and even when you do find the right one it may not work every single night. But over time you will find what works for you, start to build your confidence and eventually become a good sleeper. Trust me, everyone *can* become a good sleeper. If I can, anyone can.

If sleep is a problem for you, chances are you've never had a proper bedtime routine before, at least not formally. The plan here is to make changes to your routine that will lead to you taking charge of your sleeping patterns.

'A ruffled mind makes a restless pillow.'
— CHARLOTTE BRONTË

Here is a list of things you *should* do if you want a good night's sleep:

- Have a warm shower prior to going to bed.
- Use a dim light for reading (printed books are better than screens).
- Make sure your bedroom is a comfortable temperature and as dark as possible (hang a sheet over the window if you need to).

- Write down any issues you need to deal with the next day, which means you can then forget about them.
- If you sleep in a noisy environment, consider getting a white-noise machine.
- Write down three things you're grateful for that happened that day; gratitude is important.
- If you struggle with thoughts spinning around in your head, try to learn meditation; the Insight Timer app is effective, as well as the Calm or Headspace apps.
- Know that missing some sleep is not the end of the world. Many people have won gold medals after not sleeping the night before.
- Try to convince yourself that you're a good sleeper, and that implementing these changes is going to make a real difference to your life.

And here is a list of things you should *not* do if you want a good night's sleep:

- Don't use bright screens within thirty minutes of bedtime; this includes TV, phone, tablet.
- Avoid alcohol; it is a stimulant and will lead to many trips to the loo during the night.
- Avoid caffeine drinks after lunchtime. Caffeine has a half-life of around six hours and is still at half strength six hours after drinking.
- Don't tell yourself you're a bad sleeper. There is a good sleeper inside you; you just need to help yourself find them.

- Don't count how many hours sleep you will get if you pass out right *now*. This will do nothing but increase your anxiety.
- Don't have a visible clock in the bedroom. If you need an alarm clock, cover the face. There is nothing worse than counting down the number of hours available for sleep before your alarm goes off.

Dr Andrew Weil has developed the 4-7-8 breathing technique. It's a useful place to start, and it can put you to sleep within sixty seconds if done correctly. If it doesn't send you off to sleep it can still bring a sense of calm to your body, which will assist you greatly in falling asleep. This technique has helped me, and I recommend that you try it, too:

1. Exhale completely, making a whooshing sound through pursed lips.
2. Close your mouth and inhale quietly through your nose to a mental count of 4.
3. Hold your breath for a count of 7.
4. Exhale completely through your mouth again, making the whooshing sound to a count of 8.
5. This cycle is one breath; now inhale again and repeat the cycle 3 more times for a total of 4 breaths.

Dr Weil emphasises that the most important part of this process is holding your breath for seven seconds. This is because keeping the breath in will allow oxygen to fill your lungs and then circulate throughout your body. It's this action process that will produce a relaxing effect in your body.

Another impressive technique is to visualise painting big numbers on a large surface:

1. Imagine you're holding a paintbrush, standing in front of a large canvas.
2. Now imagine digging it into a pot of paint and painting a large number 1 in the middle of the canvas. Choose a vivid colour and be bold with your brush stroke.
3. As soon as you finish painting the 1 it disappears.
4. Now dip your brush in the paint again to start painting the number 2.
5. Repeat this process until you reach the number 10. If you make it all the way to 10, start working your way back down to 1.

If you're keen to try something even more creative, imagine you're using a calligraphy pen. Cursively write out each number, adding details and flair to each digit before it disappears, and then move on to the next number.

123456789

For those who are not readers, here are a few alternatives for customising your bedtime:

- Try listening to music, preferably something soft, relaxing and familiar.
- Colour in, in either a Can't Sleep Colour Journal or any other colouring book of your choice; this can be very peaceful and soothing.

- Use guided meditation through apps such as Insight Timer, Headspace or Calm.
- If you like to experiment with scents, there is a wide range of bedtime scent mixes available. Or come up with your own blends using lavender, chamomile, sandalwood or jasmine.
- Herbal tea about an hour before bedtime can be very relaxing (chamomile or valerian root are effective, if you can find them).
- White-noise apps can be very effective, and there are numerous options available (e.g. Sound Sleeper or White Noise).
- Keep a journal beside your bed. If you become fixated on thoughts and can't shake them, turn on the light and record what's troubling you, and then leave it until the morning to resolve.
- If you find yourself getting frustrated, get up and take a reset by getting a small drink, or going to the toilet and back to bed.
- Remove all electronic devices from your bedroom, or at least put them out of arm's reach if they need to stay in the room, making sure they're on silent and lying face down (alarms should still work even on silent but it will pay to check).
- Set your alarm for the same time every day and yes, that means no weekend sleep-in. The problem with weekend sleep-ins is that on Monday morning you've become used

to getting up later. Suddenly you have to get up at six am on Monday and you miss out on four hours of shut-eye.
- Try not to get frustrated. Remember, everyone has bad nights so try to keep calm and relaxed.

Keep at it, and hold the belief that you can be a good sleeper. It just takes time. Ensure you make sleep a priority.

CHAPTER 11

Learning to Prioritise

Have you ever created a to-do list but not known how to prioritise it? Here's a super-quick, surefire way to prioritise any list in order of the most important item to the least important.

Brainstorm everything you need to do and write the items in a list. A spreadsheet works well for this activity. Next, try to work out a rough order of priority, from most important at the top down to least important at the bottom. Then work your way down from the top. Start by asking yourself: *Is the first item more important than the second?* If not, swap them over. If it is, move to the next item on the list.

Work your way to the bottom of your list in this way. To make sure your priority list is totally correct, work your way back up again to the top. Start by asking yourself: *Is the bottom item less important than the second to bottom item?* Repeat all the way to the top.

Quick, simple, sorted. Now get cracking on your top priority.

Prioritising is such an important part of life. Things don't always go according to plan, and in these circumstances you need to adapt quickly to the changes. There just aren't the time, money or resources available to do everything. The more aware you are of your personal priorities the better you will be able to budget your money, allocate your time, and live a happy fulfilled life. Your personal values will influence your priorities in a big way and should, to a large extent, dictate how you live your life.

Prioritising your finances will help you decide if you really want that coffee or if you would rather save the five dollars for something more meaningful.

Prioritising your time will help you decide when to say no, and make you better able to guard your personal time so you recharge your batteries when you really need to.

Prioritising your values over the wants and needs of others will help you live a happy and balanced life.

CHAPTER 12

Adapting to Change

Regardless of where you work, sooner or later you're going to face change in some shape or fashion. For most people, change can be scary. I'm not going to lie: at various points in my career changes have come along that I have been frightened of. Every company I have worked for went through major takeovers—yes, *every* company. I'm talking about large-scale multibillion-dollar hostile takeovers. Not to mention restructures every twelve months, and changes of management more times than I can count.

The truth is, change impacts *everyone*, and the quicker you learn to deal with it the better you will be in the long run.

One thing I have learned over the years is that change isn't something to be fearful of. It can actually be something to get excited about. Sometimes change can lead to massive opportunities, if you have your head in the right place. Alternatively, change can lead to a downward spiral of negativity that puts you far behind your competition. It's your choice.

Each of us has a different appetite for change. Some people need overwhelming evidence that change is a positive thing before they engage in it, whereas other people chase shiny balls and are willing to embrace change just for the sake of it. Your own personal approach to change can affect others within your sphere.

KÜBLER-ROSS MODEL

It's important to understand the emotional phases we all go through when dealing with change. One model that is important to understand is Elizabeth Kübler-Ross's theory on change. While it was initially developed for dealing with grief, loss or death, it has been successfully adapted to show how people deal with all change events. I should point out that the original grief model had five stages. The general change model has been simplified, but it still assumes that each individual will go through four main stages.

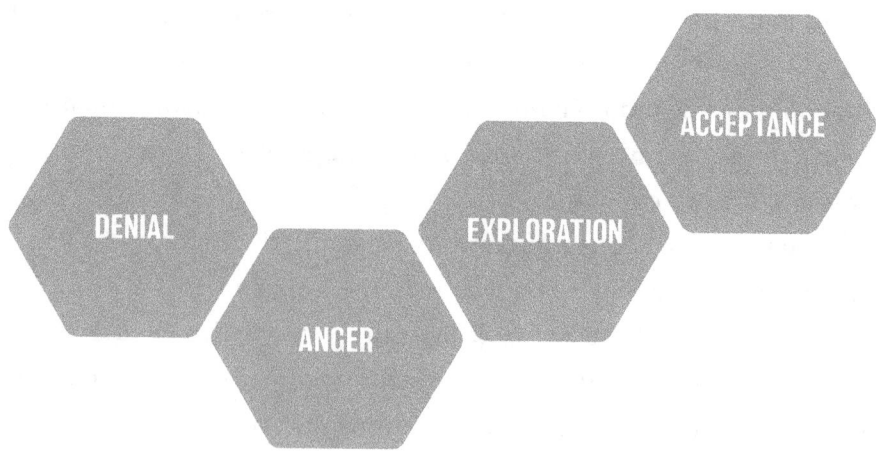

For instance, if you hear that a competitor has placed a binding offer on your company, you could react by saying:

- *No, they can't do that. How is this even possible?* (Denial)
- *Who do they think they are?* (Anger)
- *Wow, I wonder what the combined companies will look like.* (Exploring)
- *I can see some great opportunities in working for the greater combined entity.* (Acceptance)

This is not always a linear transition. You may bounce back and forward through these stages as new information comes to light, for example, from anger to exploring back to anger and finally to exploring again, before moving to acceptance.

Take a moment to reflect on a change that you have gone through in the past. Can you relate to any of these four stages? Now reflect on your ability to pass through these stages. Imagine if it took you months to pass through each stage, feeling completely lost and unaware of why you're in denial or feeling angry. Imagine that just by being aware of this model you could accelerate the process and go straight to exploring and acceptance within a week? How much better off would you be if you were on board for the change and looking towards the future?

From the model it's quite clear that the best course of action is to pass through the stages and get to acceptance as soon as possible, but how do you do this? The good news is that by simply being aware of the model, you're a long way ahead of where you would be if you'd never heard of it. You now have a flowchart that helps you feel completely justified in reacting with denial or anger towards the change that has been imposed upon you. You can also start to look at ways to transition through these stages of denial and anger more quickly by focussing on acceptance.

CORPORATE CHANGE

Corporate change can manifest in many different ways, from a company takeover, downsizing, restructure, mergers and acquisitions through to your boss simply moving on, or you rotating roles on a graduate-rotation program. When a change is inflicted upon you, you should always try to prepare as best you can. With a clear head, you need to assess the landscape and do what you can to prepare for the road ahead.

Rereading this chapter in a time of corporate change is a great way to start, so read it now, and then tuck it away for when the need arises.

If you find that you're stuck in denial, sometimes the best way to move forward is to step back and look at the big picture. *Yes, there is a big change occurring. No, you cannot change it.* Try to look objectively at what the old way looked like and how the new way is likely to look.

Knowing that anger is the next likely step, you might say to yourself: *I don't want to get angry over this. I need to accept the change, get used to it and move on. I want to move towards acceptance as soon as possible.* Try to visualise what you will feel and look like when you're in this acceptance stage. Trying to find positives from the situation will help you get to acceptance much faster.

Asking yourself who you want to be through this change process is an appropriately powerful technique. Try to aim for answers: calm, relaxed, in control, opportunistic, optimistic.

Ask yourself a few questions:

- *How can I impact what is happening?*
- *How would my best self handle this situation?*
- *In three months will I still be concerned about this?*
- *Who is in control of my emotions?*
- *What can I do to move towards accepting this change?*
- *What are the positives that will come from this change?*

Being stuck in the anger zone is no fun for you or anyone else around you. It can create a toxic environment and destroy cultures along with organisations. The key here is to remember Buddha's words: *'Holding onto anger is like drinking poison and expecting the other person to die'*.

'Grant me the serenity to accept the things I cannot change, the courage to change the things I can and the wisdom to know the difference.'

—REINHOLD NIEBUHR

In nearly all corporate-change environments, inevitably there will be water-cooler speculations on the departments to be downsized. *I heard that there were going to be ten redundancies. I heard that the new owners are going to come through and slash and burn.* It's always a good idea to keep informed, but don't get drawn into this negative gossiping. Nearly all the chatter will be coming from people in the denial and anger stages. If you've moved past this stage you'll naturally find yourself not wanting to associate with this kind of negativity, and management will notice.

Both good and bad changes result from corporate change. If your company is looking to downsize, it's best if you don't appear lazy, unmotivated or down in the dumps. This can be a perfect opportunity to put your reframing skills to good use. Sure, it might be a really hellish time around the office, but there are positives that you can look for, and opportunities you can take advantage of by putting yourself in the right place.

Here are a few examples of taking the initiative to look good in a corporate-change environment:

- Understand how you're feeling and work through the stages of denial and anger as quickly as possible. Simply knowing that you will end up at acceptance can mean you're able to skip through all the anger. Telling yourself it's going to happen anyway so you may as well get on board will be *hugely* powerful.
- Your boss is probably overloaded, so offer your assistance with anything you can do to reduce their workload.
- Try to understand the vision of what the change will look like in the future.
- Put up your hand to help make the future vision of the change a reality. This can be a brilliant opportunity to stand out from the crowd. Just imagine if the entire office is down in the dumps, in denial and angry, and you're offering to help take the new company forward.
- Step up and mentor some of the younger members in your team. Show them the Kübler-Ross model and discuss how they're feeling. This will show leadership.
- Don't waste your energy fixating on decisions that are outside of your control. Your energy can be so much better utilised shaping your future in the new world.

Change managers use a little mantra when 'stuff' happens: 'Respond; don't react'. This approach emphasises positive action in overcoming and moving forward, as opposed to a passive, woe-is-me approach.

Here are some common situations and a few tips for dealing with them:

- New manager:
    ~ Try to learn as much as you can from the departing manager. Being involved with the handover can make you a valuable asset to the new manager.
    ~ The incoming manager may know less than you do about your department, thereby making you more valuable.
    ~ The new manager may be better than the last, so give them a chance.

- New department:
    ~ Try to engage with the new team before you rotate in.
    ~ Build up a good handover report for the team you're departing.
    ~ Learn to accept that a rotation will expose you to new elements of the business. You may enjoy it more than you expect.

- Corporate takeover/acquisition/merger:
    ~ Remember that your anger won't change the situation.
    ~ Visualise what the future combined business will look like, and take advantage of any opportunities.

- ~ Remember that companies rarely buy other companies to shut them down.

- Leaving the company:
  - ~ Develop a detailed handover report, even if your replacement hasn't started yet. Put adequate time and effort into this because it will be how you're remembered within the organisation.
  - ~ Understand that others will go through the denial, anger, exploring and acceptance stages when hearing your news. This is perfectly natural so don't be offended.

At the end of the day, if it all goes pear-shaped and you end up being made redundant, there can still be great opportunities. I hope you can take the lessons from this survival guide to help yourself and those around you. This is what true leadership is all about.

Throughout this section I have condensed years of hard-won lessons into a few short chapters, effectively giving you a suitcase full of tools to use on your own journey. I have delved further into who you are as a person, what motivates you, how you can strive with confidence, and recognise what your strengths are. I've covered stress and how to manage it, how to switch off from it, and how to get a good night's sleep. I've covered prioritisation and adapting to change.

Now it's time to strap on your running shoes, discover some new ways to improve your performance and get you to where you want to be faster.

PART 3
ACCELERATE YOUR JOURNEY

CHAPTER 13

The Execution

Now it's time for you to learn how to become a high performer—and get to that point quickly. Now that you've discovered who you are and where you want to go, using some impactful tools along the way, let's step up the pace a little.

Being a high performer is about getting things done as efficiently and economically as possible. The following chapters are all about moving the needle, picking up the pace, and taking your life and career further, faster. I'll look at high-performance habits, and how you can take your life and career to the next level. I'll also reflect on professional athletes, successful business people, and a few other key high performers. I will share insights that you can use to create your own superpowers. Developing your focus and attention, and increasing your efficiency, will help you reach your goal ASAP.

I will highlight the ways in which you can set a faster pace, avoid the dead ends, perform like an elite athlete, and learn a few life hacks along the way.

In every industry there are individuals who stand out from the crowd. They have that something special that helps them achieve greatness. These people have an innate superpower, if you will.

So what are these superpowers that help them achieve more, raise the bar and ascend to greatness? There is no silver bullet; no one trait that you can learn because, unfortunately, every industry is different. The good news is that it doesn't matter if you're an introvert or an extravert; there are many paths to defining your greatness.

TIPS FROM THE PROS

Dean Ferris is a three times Australian National Pro Motocross champion. Early in his career he spent time at the Australian Institute of Sport (AIS). He has raced across Australia; in 2018 he managed the first clean sweep, winning all ten rounds of the 2018 Australian Motocross Championship. Yes, the guy is *superfast* on a dirt bike. He also has a storied international career in Europe and the United States.

I was fortunate enough to tag along to a coaching session that Dean was running, and over the course of the day he pointed out many tips that helped me improve my personal riding. I have bundled up a few of these tips with the aim of helping you take your life and career further, faster. I hope the following pointers show you how you can apply them to your own life:

- If you blow a corner, forget it straightaway. Don't take that negativity into the next corner or I guarantee you will blow that one as well. Don't let one bad corner ruin your whole race. Don't hold onto the negative things that happen to you. You need to be able to look forward positively. One bad experience needn't ruin your whole day.

- When Dean said to me, 'Worrying is wasted time', he was quoting Oprah Winfrey (not what I was expecting on a motocross track) and the advice is spot on. Worrying won't help you with anything. It will just consume energy that would be better spent solving the problem you're worrying about.

- Don't stress about sleep. When I asked Dean how he slept the night before a big event, he said he slept well all the time and that big events didn't faze him that much. While at the AIS he learned that it takes over twenty hours for a sleepless night to catch up with you, so it's highly likely the event will be over by the time any sleep deprivation impacts your performance. Knowing this should help you reduce any anxiety about not getting enough sleep, and help you fall asleep more easily. Many Olympic athletes have had sleepless nights and performed well the next day, and so can you.

- Practise good technique everywhere, including when you're riding down to the track. You don't see pro riders riding around looking sloppy; they use perfect technique all the time. Quality means doing the right thing, even when no one is watching. Make your work the highest quality, even when no one is looking. Make it a habit.

- Learn from the pros. Get a video of a pro and a video of yourself, and compare the two, taking note of the differences. Copy the pro's technique. This can be applied to many facets of life. For example, if you want to learn public speaking, study someone who is good at it. Video yourself and learn from watching it. If you want to learn to play golf, do the same.

CHAPTER 14

Routines and Habits

Routines and habits are the crux of high performance. Read that sentence again and let it sink in. If you wanted to compete against Dean Ferris in a motocross race, what would you do differently in your daily routine? Now take that same mentality and ask yourself what you would do if you wanted to compete against (and beat) the elite people in your industry.

People at the top of their game don't roll out of bed after hitting the snooze button twice, stagger into the shower, get dressed, and drive off to work each morning. No, they are *motivated*. They set the alarm, and when it goes off they're out of bed and on their way. They fuel their bodies, train, and get coaching from the best coaches. They invest in themselves, and have an unwavering mindset that tells them they are there to do their life's work.

Here are some super-simple additions to add to your morning routine:

- Don't hit the snooze button, *ever*. Count 5, 4, 3, 2, 1 and get up. (Look up Mel Robbins' 5-second rule on YouTube, or read her book, *The 5 Second Rule*.)
- Head straight to the kitchen and drink a minimum of 500 millilitres of water to start rehydrating your body, replenishing what you have lost through the night.
- When you're in the shower, ask yourself the following:
  - *Who do I want to be today?*
  - *What are my top three goals for today?*
  - *Which parts of today are going to be great?*
  - *What can I be grateful for today?*
- Eat a nutritious breakfast that will fuel your body.
- Do a mindfulness guided meditation, or try practising gratitude.
- Pack a healthy lunch and snacks that will keep your energy levels steady throughout the day.

Here are a few tips to get you through your workday:

- Plan your day. Always block out time on Monday morning to plan your week.
- Focus on one task at a time.
- Get into flow states throughout the day (more on this in the next chapter).
- Block out time in your calendar to focus on key tasks.
- Take a short reset every hour; this is non-negotiable.

CHAPTER 15

Flow States

A flow state is a trance-like state where the brain actively taps into the conscious and subconscious processors. Being in a flow state allows you to have incredible focus on the task at hand. It will improve your performance *and* your cognitive abilities.

Have you ever found yourself in a state of mind where your surroundings seem to fade away until there are no distractions, and everything just seems to click? If you write a report in this state, the words flow effortlessly; there is structure, ease and high output with minimal effort. This is known as a flow state and once you learn how to slide in and out of this state your productivity will skyrocket. (This phenomenon has been covered in many books, including *Deep Learning* by Cal Newport, and *Stealing Fire* by Steven Kotler and Jamie Wheal.)

There are some clear parameters around flow states. You can't click your fingers and just go in and out of flow. It's not that simple.

Sometimes you can just fall into it, but at other times you can never find it. This is why you need to develop a system or framework to increase your chances of at least partially getting into flow.

Being in a flow state means not only utilising your conscious mind but also tapping into your subconscious mind. In everyday life outside of flow, when you're concentrating on a task you're in a conscious state of mind. You're actively thinking about what you're doing. This conscious state uses around five percent of your mental capacity.

You may have heard that the subconscious mind is so much more powerful than the conscious mind, which explains why you often solve weighty problems when you're not even consciously thinking about them or trying to find a solution. Flow states allow you to blur the line between the conscious and subconscious, and use both simultaneously, effectively unlocking the greater potential of your full brain. It's easy to see why it's a good place to be.

Neuroscientists from the Defence Advanced Research Project Agency (DARPA) report that being in a flow state can help to achieve a 500-percent increase in productivity, or up to a 490-percent increase in skill acquisition. These are amazing claims, but I have faith in the statistics.

Marines are taught entire new languages in a matter of weeks, rather than the usual 6-month timeframe. These flow states are also critically important when marines are completing missions, when the entire squadron is in sync and everyone instinctively knows what to do. Every marine in the squadron is one hundred percent in the moment, focused entirely on the job at hand.

Sporting teams provide another example. A player is out on the field, completely immersed in the game, completely oblivious to who is sitting on the sidelines. They're in the zone. Their conscious brain is picking away at the movements of the game. They're completely in sync with their subconscious brain, which brings all their training and skills to the table. They feel as though everything clicks, and time floats by as though they're in their own little world. When an entire team is in sync, that's when massive upsets happen on the playing field: the underdogs take down the top side purely by playing as a synchronous team.

To those who have experienced this phenomenon, great, you know what I'm talking about, and chances are you would love to be shown how to achieve this again, in a repeatable way.

If you've never experienced the phenomenon, you're probably thinking that the concept sounds crazy and I should get back to helping you with your life and career. But hear me out.

Fair warning: getting into a flow state does trigger a fairly intense release of serotonin and dopamine. Trying to stay in this state for too long can become draining and potentially lead to burnout. Generally, I don't recommend any longer than 45–50 minutes in a flow state before transitioning out, taking a reset then transitioning back in. Trust me, it's worth it. The increased productivity during this time far outweighs the short breaks required.

It's important to note that you must focus one hundred percent on one thing at a time. This is one of the key pillars of high performance. Put simply, your brain cannot multitask, so don't expect it to. If you have five tasks you want to achieve for the day, allocate a block of time for each individual task, with a small break between them. Your task is to then go into an individual flow state for each of these tasks.

Use the following structure as a guide to getting yourself into a flow state:

Stage 1: Planning

It's all about preparation. Plan your task, do your research, and have everything you need at your fingertips. Set up your environment for success: have some water at hand and try to eliminate distractions. A silly little distraction can break you out of flow in an instant. For example, you're typing away at a million miles an hour and the flight attendant asks if you'd like a drink of water. Bam! Flow gone. *Where was I? What was I writing about?*

Be aware of the distractions that are lying in wait. Turn off your emails, put your phone face down, on silent, or better yet, on airplane mode.

Use headphones as a do-not-disturb sign. You will likely find that people stop tapping you on the shoulder if you're wearing headphones, even if you're not listening to anything. If you do listen to music, make sure it's upbeat and familiar. Don't play new music, and try to make sure the tone of the music is in line with the flow state you want to be in. New music takes up too much brain capacity and you'll find yourself trying to learn the new lyrics or figure out what the song is all about. I have a few different playlists set up that help me get into flow, depending on what tasks I'm focusing on.

Key reminders for planning: do your research, eliminate all distractions, and focus on one task at a time. The book *Indistractable* by Nir Eyal is an excellent guide for eliminating distractions.

Stage 2: Relax

Step away from the task at hand and switch off from it. That means no screen time and no social media. Read a book, meditate, or go for a brief walk and do a reset when you come back and sit down. Try to allocate at least five minutes for this. It might seem like a waste of time when you need to be getting into the task, but this clarity will help you to focus one hundred percent on the task at hand.

Stage 3: Get into flow

This is the tricky stage. You're prepared and relaxed, and now you have to get into flow, but once you've mastered going into flow it's actually quite easy. Tips for the steps to take when you're writing a report, email or blog:

1. Jot down a few bullet points to frame what you want to talk about.
2. Start padding out these bullet points. It's important to overcome procrastination before it starts, so just start anywhere.
3. When you start typing, try to zone out. You should become lost in the words and enter a meditative state where everything just flows
4. Ignore, or turn off, automatic spelling-error notifications. You want to stay in the flow to keep the story going inside your head, not going back up the page to fix spelling or grammar errors. You can always correct these later.

You'll know when you've entered a flow state. You'll reach a point where your fingers can't keep up with your brain.

If you struggle with using a computer, try writing things down longhand. This can help to slow the brain down a little (I can generally write longhand far longer than I can type on a computer).

There are lots of other options, too. For example, there are some useful software packages that will convert your recorded voice to text. Try recording whatever comes out of your mouth. Lie down in a dark room with your eyes shut, with zero distractions, and talk to your heart's content. Let it flow.

Stage 4: Recovery

When you've been in a hyper-productive state, it's important to take time out afterwards to let it all cool down. You don't want to stay in the flow zone until you just start to 'wander' out of it. It's much better to stop, recover, and then start the cycle again. (When re-entering the flow state, you can generally skip the first stage unless you need to do more research.)

Recovery is important. It's essential that you step away from the flow state and try to get it out of your head for a while. Try doing some exercise, or a meditation, or find someone to talk to. Do anything that takes your attention away from what you were doing.

The main idea here is that you get into flow and have high-intensity sessions three or four times per day. It takes practice and time—along with a bit of trial and error—to find what works best for you. Imagine if someone had taught you this technique in high school.

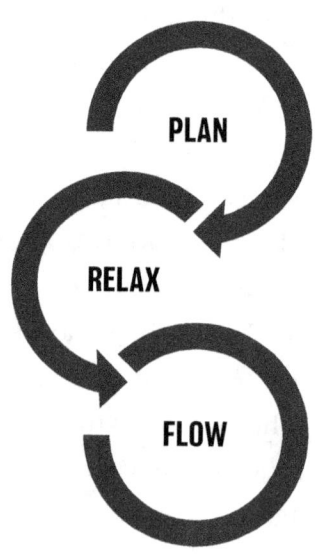

Even if you increase you daily productivity by only twenty percent, this could equate to you saving ninety-six minutes over an 8-hour workday. You could use these ninety-six minutes to work on more value-added activities, or personal development, or to go home early because you've finished everything required of you. (More likely it will allow you to leave on time instead of staying back to get everything done.)

Focusing on one task at a time with no distractions *will* lead to a massive natural boost in your productivity. Start by planning your day, allocate time for each of your key tasks, and get to it.

CHAPTER 16

Multitasking

Multitasking is a myth. The more you try to multitask, the quicker you burn your energy, and the quicker you deplete and crash out. When you attempt to multitask, what you're actually doing is rapidly switching focus from one activity to another in a process called cognitive switching. This switching comes at a cost.

To elaborate further, consider a single-core computer processor versus a multi-core processor. The former needs to switch between processes, but the latter can allocate tasks to each additional core. The human brain is a single-core processor, which means you need to be mindful of how many activities you're trying to accomplish at the same time, for instance, trying to write an email while you're talking on the phone.

ONE THING AT A TIME + 100-PERCENT FOCUS = GETTING MORE DONE

Doing one thing at a time means you work efficiently, effectively, and to your full potential. Trying to do multiple things at once will lead to you doing *none* of them to your full potential. From an energy perspective, rapid switching from task to task is incredibly taxing. You'll find you need to take more regular breaks, and you'll often run out of energy at the end of the day.

People constantly argue this point with me, claiming that they can breathe, walk and talk at the same time. Sure, it's possible to do multiple primal functions simultaneously; these internal systems effectively manage themselves. But when it comes to complex external tasks, you're far better off focusing on one thing at a time.

It might help to make things clearer if I explain the multitasking myth in a slightly different way. Yes, you can talk on the phone, answer an email, and try to juggle at the same time. Ultimately your brain is bouncing really fast from one task to the other, covering all three activities, yet only focusing on one at a time. But if you continue to try to do all three things at once, chances are that you will lose track of the conversation, make a mistake in the email, and drop your juggling balls.

So eliminate distractions. Find your flow state. Crush it!

Essentially, your brain has a set bandwidth, and when you exceed the available bandwidth things will start to crash. Listening to familiar music, for instance, may take up ten percent of your bandwidth; however, if listening to that music helps to avoid distractions that might take up fifty percent of your brain's bandwidth, this would be considered a good investment.

Multitasking should only ever be considered for low-level tasks. Juggling might take sixty percent of your bandwidth, while holding a conversation may take fifty percent. Trying to do both at the same time might lead to you dropping the balls and missing the conversation.

The good thing is that with practice and repetition, your actions will become habitual. For instance, juggling may initially take ninety percent of your brain's bandwidth, but as you get better this figure will drop. You could get to a point where you can juggle and keep a conversation going at the same time, although it would be taxing on the brain.

Yes, you can switch between juggling and conversation with enough practice, but you'll be robbing the conversation of your full attention.

If you're keen to learn more about habits, there are two books I highly recommend: *Atomic Habits* by James Clear, and *High Performance Habits* by Brendon Burchard.

CHAPTER 17

Procrastination

In this chapter I offer some critical tips to help you crush procrastination. There is a theory in which all the dull jobs you don't want to do are referred to as frogs. Mark Twain once said, 'If it's your job to eat a frog, it's best to do it first thing in the morning. And if it's your job to eat two frogs, it's best to eat the biggest one first.' So there you go, eat the frogs first thing and you can enjoy the rest of your day doing the tasks you get some joy from.

Another popular method for curing procrastination and the dreaded writer's block (this tip has been ever so helpful in writing this book) is to create a habit of starting *anywhere*. The theory goes that by immersing yourself in the task, jotting down a few points, or a bullet here or there, or sketching notes, this will get the creative juices flowing. Before you know it you will start to fall into a flow state.

As mentioned earlier, Mel Robbins wrote a popular book called *The 5 Second Rule*. Simply put, the rule is a 5-second countdown timer. For example, if you're struggling to get out of bed on time, when you hear the alarm go off count down 'five–four–three–two–one', then throw off the covers and get up before you have a chance to think about it.

According to Robbins, the 5-second rule works because it doesn't give your conscious brain time to come up with excuses for why this is a bad idea. When you start to overthink, things become harder. If you're standing at the top step of the diving board, trying to overcome the fear, count down 'five–four–three–two–one' and jump. Don't overthink it. This one really works. (Check out the book or watch one of the author's YouTube clips.)

This technique is obviously very useful when getting out of bed in the morning, but it's also effective for overcoming any type of procrastination, or taking a leap outside your comfort zone.

Some people have found success with the Pomodoro method, which was developed by Francesco Cirillo in the late 1980s (*pomodoro* is the Italian word for tomato). The Pomodoro Technique garnered its name when Francesco used a cheap tomato timer set to twenty-five minutes (you can use whatever timer you like).

This is how it works: you sit down and focus on one task for twenty-five minutes, forcing yourself to concentrate on being productive until those twenty-five minutes are up. You then take a 5-minute break before resetting the timer and going again. After four rounds of 5-minute breaks, you take a longer break, ideally around thirty minutes.

If you get distracted during a 25-minute session, jot down the distraction on a notepad and tend to it later in the day. Eliminating distractions and focusing on one task at a time are the keys to success with this technique.

Personally, I have found the Pomodoro Technique to be both good and bad. Adding time pressure can introduce a sense of performance anxiety. I have had times where the additional time pressure has led to a case of writer's block, and I haven't appreciated the additional stress. Conversely, the time pressure could help you snap into the zone and perform at a higher level much more quickly.

Like anything, the technique takes practice. The more comfortable you become with it, the better your results will be. Try the Pomodoro Technique for yourself and see how it goes.

A big part of getting past procrastination is having the right mindset; once you believe you can overcome this block, it will diminish until it no longer exists. Asking yourself the right questions is an efficient way to get into the right mindset.

CHAPTER 18

Asking the Right Questions

Just ask Brendon Burchard or Tony Robbins, the top two high-performance coaches in the world, about the power of asking the right questions and they will throw hundreds of examples at you.

In my opinion, there are two main keys to successfully asking questions: knowing the right questions to ask, and knowing what the wrong questions are. Simply put, you need to reframe bad questions into good ones. For instance, when something negative happens, don't ask: *Why is this happening to me?* Instead, ask: *What can I learn from this?*

Helpful questions you could ask yourself on a daily basis:

- *Who do I want to be today?*

- *What do I want to achieve today?*
- *What can I be grateful for?*
- *Where can I add value?*
- *Who do I want to be when I walk into this meeting?*
- *How can I improve on this and do it better next time?*
- *When I get home from work today, who do I want to be when I walk into the house?*

Here is a list of unhelpful questions, and suggestions for reframing them:

UNHELPFUL QUESTIONS	REFRAMING UNHELPFUL QUESTIONS
Why is this happening to me?	What can I learn from this?
What makes them more special than me?	How am I stronger than them?
Why is everything such a mess?	How can I take control of this situation?
Can I give up yet?	What does success look like?

Being aware of the questions that constantly spin around inside your mind is the first step to cracking the code to reframing these questions. Have you ever met a person who is forever the optimist, the kind of person who can see the good in every situation? Setbacks seem to slide right off them as they plough forward with ambition and intent. This is the mindset to emulate to achieve your goals in life, and the best way to get there is to start asking yourself the *right* questions.

Rather than hammer home the message that asking the right

questions will give you some sort of innate superpower, I prefer to frame it as a question: *How would my best self handle this situation?* When you set yourself a challenge to handle a situation to the best of your abilities, that's when you will start reaching your fullest potential.

Now that we're asking the right questions, it's time to speed things up a little.

CHAPTER 10

Learning to Read Faster

Imagine if you could read this book in three hours instead of six. What could you do with that spare three hours? Learning to read a little faster can be a massive game changer to the volume of content you can consume. The more content you consume (and retain) the more value you can add.

'The more that you read, the more things you will know.
The more that you learn, the more places you'll go.'
—DR SEUSS

One of the training courses I have completed is Jim Kwik's free speed-reading webinar, which contains some excellent tips on how to take your reading to the next level. I'm pleased to say that from the tips I picked up from this one-hour course, I managed to increase my reading speed from 290 words per minute to around 410 words per minute. This 40-percent increase in speed alone was greatly beneficial, but I also found that it actually helped me concentrate better. I was able to avoid rereading sections, and I didn't get distracted nearly as much as I normally would have.

The standout tip for me was to follow my finger. Yes, that's going back to how we were taught in primary school. Follow your finger. Your eyes are more attracted to motion than a sheet of paper. Try this technique for yourself in the following pages of this book.

How to work out how many words per minute you can read:

1. Set a timer for one minute and read as many lines as you can of any book. Mark where you start and finish, and then count the words you read in that time (counting the number of words on an average line and multiplying that by the number of lines will give you a close enough result).
2. Set the timer again, and this time follow your finger, moving your finger as fast as you can keep up with it. Count the number of words you've read using the method above.
3. Calculate your improvement. My initial score was 290 words per minute, and this increased to 410 words per minute. I calculated this with the following formula: (410-290)/290 = a 41.3-percent increase in words per minute).

If you're keen to see if you can achieve a similar increase in your reading speed I recommend you follow Jim Kwik and check out his free courses at https://kwikbrain.com/speedreading.

Use this QR code to access the Kwik speed reading course.

I generally get through one book every two weeks, approximately twenty-six books a year. With this speed increase, my yearly reading list should increase by twelve books. Taking into account that I can now read with fewer distractions, and read for longer durations without repeating sections, it will likely double.

The same can be done for audiobooks and podcasts. Increasing the playback speed will keep your mind focussed on the material and avoid drifting off while listening.

Remember, learners are earners. The more you know, the more value you can bring to your organisation, and the more value you bring, the quicker you accelerate your career.

CHAPTER 20

Career Progression

The impact of becoming a high performer in your chosen career can be powerful. Compare a high performer with an average performer, with both starting on a salary of $50,000 per year. If the high performer were to outperform their counterpart by achieving an additional 5-percent pay rise each year (let's say a 2-percent pay rise versus a 7-percent pay rise) the compounded impact over the next forty years of their working career would be astounding.

I have crunched the numbers for you. After forty working years, the average performer would be on approximately $108,237 per year. Not bad. This means they would have doubled their salary.

The high performer, however, would be on a whopping $699,741 per year. Yes, an annual $591,000 more than the average performer at the forty-year mark.

Over their working lives, the average performer would earn a tidy $3.02 million.

The high performer would earn $9.98 million.

Are you willing to leave that $591,000 per year, or that $6.96 million on the table over the course of your career?

YEAR	2-PERCENT INCREASE	7-PERCENT INCREASE
1	$50,000	$50,000
2	$51,000	$53,500
3	$52,020	$57,245
4	$53,060	$61,252
5	$54,122	$65,540
6	$56,308	$70,128
7	$56,308	$75,037
8	$57,434	$80,289
9	$58,583	$85,909
10	$59,755	$91,923
30	$88,792	$355,713
40	$108,237	$699,741
TOTAL	**$3,020,099**	**$9,981,756**

The prize is potentially immense—if you take an interest in your career and follow the steps set out in this book to make yourself a high performer. You might think these figures are totally unachievable, but let me give you some statistics from my own story.

At the age of twenty-three I landed my first full-time role. By the age of twenty-five I had doubled my salary. By the age of twenty-eight I had doubled it again. At age twenty-nine I received a 34-percent pay rise on my already good base pay. Yes, this pay rise was 1.5 times my starting salary six years earlier. By the time I was thirty-three my dividend payments coming in from investments were greater than my starting salary ten years earlier.

I'm not saying that this is what everyone wants, but it does go to show that if you're willing to create goals and apply yourself one hundred percent to achieving them, nearly anything is possible.

So, how do you become a high performer in your chosen career? It's simple, really. All it takes is a bit of time and effort, along with a vision of what you want to achieve and some dedication to your craft.

CAREER-LIMITING MOVES

We have established that there are ways to help you get to the top. It goes without saying that there are other ways that will see red marks placed against your name.

At one point in my career I very nearly lost my job for swearing 'emphatically' at one of my employees after a particularly bad misstep on their part. After being asked by the employee not to swear, I lost it and did exactly that. An hour later I was being roasted by HR about how I needed coaching on how to handle these situations, which, to be honest, I probably did. After I explained that a document had been fraudulently filled out and we were facing a $750,000 delay charge, HR calmed down and swung to my side of the argument (thankfully I had a good relationship with the HR manager). The matter was resolved amicably and everyone moved on to get the job done.

Lesson learned: don't swear at your employees, no matter how badly they stuff up.

Here are some of the other career-limiting moves I have witnessed over my career:

- Hooking up with a workmate at a work Christmas party
- Fraudulent behaviour and falsification of documentation
- Racially unacceptable slurs and comments leading to multiple dismissals
- Printing personal documents at work and leaving them on the printer for all to see
- Sexual discrimination and/or harassment
- Inappropriate emails sent to and from work email addresses
- Inappropriate use of corporate credit cards
- Inappropriate use of instant-messaging networks
- Badmouthing someone's boss while the boss was standing over the recipient's shoulder
- Someone introducing themselves to the CEO after a few too many drinks at a work function (there is nothing like slurring your words through some Dutch courage)

Remember, a bad reputation will last much longer than memories of the good things you have done.

But you're not here to limit your career. In the next chapter I cover some of the key aspects that are critical to you taking your career further, faster.

CHAPTER 21

From Technician to Manager to Leader

As we've seen in the previous chapters, there is a natural transition you will make from technician to manager to leader, if you choose to do so. The best way to go about transcending these stages is to study upwards. What skills do the people on the next level have that you need to develop?

Transitioning from technician to manager may require you to acquire people-management skills, or more business acumen. It's a common misconception that you need to study for an MBA to become a manager, which simply isn't the case. Don't get me wrong, an MBA is a valuable piece of education, but it's not an absolute requirement for becoming a good manager or leader.

If you want a good overview of the content of an MBA, I recommend you check out *The Personal MBA* by Josh Kaufman. If you like the content in this book, and you have the time, resources and desire, by all means go ahead and do an MBA. But generally I advise people to wait until they have at least five to ten years' experience before tackling this qualification.

One of the most influential factors involved in becoming a good manager or leader is your capacity to be empathetic towards your workers. You need to learn what makes them tick, and what their drivers and values are. Once you know why your workers are there, you can help to engage them in the right way. You can find ways to motivate them intrinsically. This often comes down to having high emotional intelligence (for some thorough insights into the world of emotional intelligence, I recommend *Emotional Intelligence* by Daniel Goleman). As a general rule:

- The role of the technician is to look days to weeks ahead. Their manager will line up the work they want done and the technician will diligently go about processing that work.
- The role of a manager is to keep the technicians busy, looking weeks, months and possibly a year ahead to ensure they have sufficient technicians to achieve the short-term goals of the company. From a motivational perspective, a manager should motivate the technicians to achieve the work required. Again, aim for intrinsic rather than extrinsic motivation.
- The role of a leader is to look at least one to five years ahead and predict where the company needs to go. A leader should inspire the entire organisation to pursue his or her vision of where the organisation should head.

A constructive way for you to prepare for the next stage is to start looking further ahead. When you start accurately predicting where your team needs to be on the next horizon, you're placing yourself in a favourable position to take the next step.

A powerful way to be seen as a leader is to become a prominent person within your industry.

CHAPTER 22

Becoming a Prominent Person in Your Industry

In every industry, there are a few who become prominent key figures. These are generally the people who make it to the top, who get paid the most. They are also the people with the most influence who actually get to shape an industry. They are the twenty percent from the 80/20 rule: the wealthiest twenty percent earns more than eighty percent of the world's income.

There are a number of key things to note about becoming a prominent figure in your industry. You must be prepared to put yourself out there. Meet people and connect. Get involved in the industry.

Update your LinkedIn profile, and be *visible*. Even if you don't post new content on LinkedIn, it can still be a useful and fruitful place to keep in touch with the rest of the industry. Make it a habit to log in to LinkedIn and like or comment on relevant posts. I'm a keen fan of LinkedIn, and whenever I meet someone in person I will always put through a connection request (with a personalised message). For some impactful advice on networking, I recommend Jordan Harbinger's free *6 minute networking* course at www.jordanharbinger.com/courses.

Use this QR code to access the Jordan Harbinger six minute networking course.

Contributing to your industry can be tricky when you're starting out, but there are ways of doing it. Firstly, you could volunteer your time on industry member boards. You could mentor younger team members or current students, and promote your industry by liking and commenting on social media posts. As you work your way up, you could start looking at writing papers, speaking on panels, and so on.

There is an art to networking in any industry. Attending networking events, training sessions and seminars are all especially effective ways to get to know others in your industry. Regardless of what type of organisation you are with, I thoroughly recommend you invest some time in developing your network. There is a truthful saying: 'Your network is your net worth.'

The goal of building a network is to foster long-term relationships. These relationships need to be mutual and beneficial to both parties. Do your best to keep in touch with the existing prominent members of your industry; their magic does rub off, even if only by association. By following in their footsteps you will begin to assert your prominence.

Above all else, be good at what you do. Apply time to mastering your craft. I strongly recommend that you find your niche and *own* it. Your goal is to become the go-to person in that space. You want to be respected enough that customers come to you rather than you having to chase them.

Daniel Priestley has written a powerful book called *Key Person of Influence*, which is worth checking out if you're keen to become an influential person in your field.

The next step is to learn impeccable negotiation skills.

CHAPTER 23

Negotiating Like a Pro

Negotiation is a skill that is often used yet seldom taught. Here are my thoughts on developing your own negotiation skills.

First of all, let's go back to basics. What is negotiation? *The Oxford Dictionary* defines negotiation as 'Discussion aimed at reaching an agreement'. We could also think of it as a method by which people settle differences. It's a way for two parties to come together and agree on a way forward.

In nearly all cases, a negotiation is an interaction where two parties exchange goods or services for a price (a swap). For negotiations to work, both parties need to be satisfied that they have received fair value from the transaction. Negotiations can be extremely straightforward and simple, or extremely long and drawn out, depending on what is at stake.

A few examples:

- Buying a cake from a bakery: This is an invitation to tender. The shop sets a price, you agree to pay the price, and the two parties exchange the cash for the cake. Simple.
- Offering a lower price on a second-hand car: This could encourage a discussion in which both parties agree on a price that is acceptable to both.
- Negotiating a construction contract valued at $250 million: This could take many months to settle out all the associated terms and conditions. Complex.

Ideally, you should always aim for a win-win outcome, where both parties walk away feeling like they have achieved a good deal. Even with a $250-million construction contract, the owner should feel that they are receiving good value, and the contractor should feel that they can achieve a desired profit margin.

Personal tip: Contractors need to make a profit. As soon as contractors start losing money they will cut corners and it *will* cost you both more in the long run.

What makes a good negotiator? Over the course of my career I have spent many, many hours negotiating contracts, from simple ones through to some of the largest construction contracts in the state of Queensland, including one valued at $270 million. And this is not including my numerous personal endeavours when buying cars, houses, bikes, and everything in between.

Here are my top ten tips for becoming a good negotiator:

1. Always have other options.
2. Do your research.
3. Be willing to walk away from a negotiation.
4. Try not to be fixated on *having* to buy a particular item, whether it's a house, car, or anything else; there are always other fish in the sea so leave yourself other options.
5. Be patient and remain calm.
6. Understand what the other person in the negotiation wants from the agreement. For example, when buying a house you might find the seller is more interested in the price than a shorter settlement period. Listen to their drivers. Once you know their drivers, you can adjust your pitch to accommodate them.
7. Don't make things personal. Remember, it's just a negotiation for an exchange of goods or services and personalities don't come into it.
8. Know what you're willing to pay or accept.
9. Try to keep emotion out of the situation. Yes, you want the item, but don't let your emotions run away with your chequebook.
10. Keep a clear head so you can think tactfully in the heat of a negotiation. If you don't feel you're getting fair value, walk away.

Building on these points, buying a house is likely to be the biggest investment you ever make. Here are my top ten tips for buying property:

1. Don't fall in love with a house before you buy it; always try to stay objective.
2. Develop key performance indicators (KPIs) on what the house needs. It could be the number of bedrooms, garage space, facilities, proximity to work, shops, public transport or even local schools.
3. If you doubt your ability to properly assess the property, seek professional advice on the condition and valuation of the property. Any defects or issues can add weight to your bargaining power.
4. Use areas of improvement and/or defects as measures to reduce the asking price.
5. Find out the drivers of the seller and try to meet their drivers. Maybe they've bought elsewhere and need a quick settlement. If so, try to offer a short settlement period. They could be older and scaling back. If so, they might want a longer settlement period.
6. Have your finances pre-approved if possible.
7. Price may not be the only driver. Show that you're a decent person looking to get into the housing market. It's also an advantage to let the seller know you have other options.
8. Don't try to make the person on the other side of the table feel like they're being backed into a corner. You will always catch more flies with honey than vinegar.
9. Never give away your position; keep your cards close to your chest.
10. Be willing to stick to your guns. Know your budget, and don't pay above that price. The right property will come along at some point in time.

The above advice can be used for many purchases, including cars, bikes, boats, or anything where negotiation is a possibility. When purchasing a car from a dealership, don't be afraid to walk out. There are many other dealerships that will be keen to do a deal. Remember to find out the car dealers' drivers; for instance, many dealerships want to get their numbers up for the month.

When making offers, never lead with your best one. You don't want to offend anyone by offering too low a price, but always keep a little up your sleeve.

In sales, there is an important rule for negotiations. When someone has made an offer, generally the first person to speak *loses* the negotiation. If you make an offer for a car that is twenty percent below the asking price, sit back and wait for the other person to respond. As soon as you follow up or ask the person on the other side what they think, they will generally reject your offer, meaning you end up paying more. You'll be in a far more commanding position if you sit back, confident that you've made a worthwhile offer.

Always 'sell' your offer. Once you know the drivers of the person you're buying from, you can tailor your offer to suit.

A few examples:

- When buying a secondhand car, you could say, 'Hi, would you be willing to accept $3000, cash in hand, for a quick, hassle-free transaction? I could come and pick it up tonight if everything is in order.' Note how you're threading the seller's drivers of a quick, hassle-free sale into your pitch.
- When buying a house, try to apply time pressure by making your offer valid for twenty-four hours only. You can also note that if the offer is not accepted you're going to pursue

alternative options. If they don't act within the timeframe and come back at a later date, you're within your rights to offer less and see if they will accept. You could say, 'We would love to make [*address*] our family home, and we're willing to place an offer of [*amount*] based on a [*time*] settlement period, as preferred by the vendor. Our offer is valid for twenty-four hours and will expire at [*time*], after which we will pursue alternate properties.'

- When bidding in an auction, a powerful technique is to increase the bid in higher increments than the current tempo. For example, if the bids are going up in $5,000 increments, offer a $10,000 or $20,000 increment (providing you're within your budget). This change in tempo can be a subtle but effective way to upset other bidders, often throwing them off guard and making them back down sooner than they may have.

Remember, in an auction you're negotiating with the other bidders. Psychology plays a big part, and jumping the price up quickly will infer that you have deep pockets and that you're willing to intimidate the competition.

SALARY NEGOTIATION

Negotiating a pay rise can be a tricky ordeal. Many times during my career I've experienced both the highs and the lows of trying to negotiate a higher salary. There are many moving parts to a successful salary-increase negotiation. Some parts are within your control but others are not. Your yearly performance review is a key factor. While it pays dividends to prepare well for these, the conversations should be occurring throughout the year.

Each year your manager should view your performance in both quantitative and qualitative ways. Quantitative is where you're measured against targets, KPIs and any points set out at the beginning of the year. Generally, you would be ranked on these quantitative elements using your internal systems (such as a rating out of 5). Most employers will encourage you to self-score these. Your boss will give their own score, and then you discuss the results. In these circumstances don't undersell yourself. Always look at it from the point of view of how someone with your years of experience should perform.

The qualitative measure is by far the softer measure. This is more about how you conduct yourself in your role, how easy you are to get along with, and how willing you are to put in some extra effort where required. How you interact with your boss and everyone else in the office plays a big part in your qualitative scoring. This is an area where many people let themselves down; for example, getting drunk at the Christmas party will have a definite impact on your qualitative score.

Remember, your manager always has a little discretion either way with your quantitative scoring; how you behave may mean the difference between 3 or 4 when it comes to your qualitative scoring.

Often budgets are quite slim for salary increases and only the people who excel will see the riches. It always pays to present yourself in the best light, and try to upsell yourself during these reviews. Gaining a few extra points here or there on your performance reviews will have a big impact on your ability to negotiate a higher salary.

Take control of the things you can control:

- Achieving your yearly goals and KPIs
- Preparing for your performance review (see the next section)
- Paying attention to your workplace persona

- Impressing your boss in the months leading up to your formal review

Be aware of the things you can't control:

- Adverse market conditions, and low profit margins
- Salary freezes
- Takeovers and acquisitions

Always keep your cool, and good luck with driving your next negotiation.

CHAPTER 24

Performance Reviews

One of the easiest and most efficient ways to accelerate your career is through preparation for your performance reviews. The proper preparation will put you in a strong position to sell all the work you have done through the year. This is not about getting something you don't deserve; it's about getting what you *do* deserve. When you perform well year after year, the results compound, you will be rewarded with quicker promotions, and a higher salary will follow.

Always prepare for your performance reviews. As you saw from the earlier example, a bigger pay rise/bonus each year compounds to impressive figures over the course of your career.

Your company will likely have a set process to follow. There will be forms to fill in and submit prior to and possibly following your review. Ensure that you're familiar with the process: dot the i's and cross the t's. If you need to handwrite the forms, use your neatest handwriting and make sure you use correct spelling and grammar—it all counts.

Make sure you keep a diary of all your achievements through the year. This diary should include how you have met each of your KPIs, where you have gone above and beyond, and how you're exceeding expectations. Try to keep a record of any tangible examples, such as times you were praised by others, won awards, or even volunteered to help the team. Review your diary before your performance review and take this evidence with you.

In my opinion, a performance review should always be two-dimensional. Half the time should be spent looking back over what you have achieved over the past twelve months, and the other half of the time should be spent looking at the future, and how you're going to develop over the coming year.

At one particular point in my career my boss and I went to great lengths to prepare for my performance review. I ended up scoring a 34-percent pay rise. Needless to say, I was already on a high salary and this increase was a life-changing experience.

Here are my top ten tips for planning for success in your next performance review:

1. Strive to thrive: Your recent work performance can have a major bearing on your review. Much like a schoolteacher only remembers your behaviour in the previous weeks, your manager's most recent memories of you will be top of mind, and will greatly influence their appraisal of you. In the weeks leading up to your review, put in that little bit of extra effort. Arrive at work earlier. Stay back later. Avoid long lunches. Cut out the water-cooler chatter. Put up your hand for more responsibilities. Ask questions. Show zeal. Reach higher.

2. Dress to impress: The previous point covered substance; this point deals with style. For your review, dress for the job you want to be in. Plan your wardrobe. Is your preferred outfit up to scratch? Popped buttons, frayed hems and scuffmarks will all diminish your overall appearance. Consider a new ensemble, or make sure your suit and shirt are cleaned, pressed and ready to go. Shine your shoes. Get a haircut. You know the drill.

3. Prepare: One of the most important things you can do to ensure the success of your performance review is to actively prepare for it. Zero prep will get you zero results, and any claim that you're too busy working is no defence. A couple of hours of preparation could lead to an extra couple of percent pay rise or bonus in your pocket. Even if the rise was only $500 this would equate to $250 per hour—perhaps the most rewarding hours of your work year.

   Good preparation is all about collating evidence of you meeting and exceeding your KPIs. Over the course of the year, keep a diary or electronic folder updated with all your achievements through the year. In the days leading up to your performance review, collate your achievements and accolades ready for your review.

   Remember, this is about informing your line manager about all the good things you have done during the year; it's not about overselling yourself.

4. Be a big note: With all this information as background, you're ready to prepare a list of your accomplishments. In a performance review, it's okay to brag a little. Your boss may not be aware of the contribution you've made or the great

things you've done. In the days leading up to the review, prepare notes covering the most important points:

- Your achievements for the year
- The times you've gone above and beyond
- The times you've filled in for a higher pay grade
- Analysis of your KPIs; develop demonstrations for where you have met each one
- Any training and development you've undertaken over the year
- Your goals for the following year; take control, and don't let your manager hand them down to you
- List of things you want to discuss in the review

5. Remember that nobody's perfect: In reviewing your annual highlights and list of accomplishments, identify any areas where you felt you struggled, or any times where your think your performance fell short. Make a note of any negative aspects of the year and come up with constructive elements from these experiences. What did you learn? How would you do things differently next time?

Identify any areas where you would like to expand your skills or competencies. Ask for coaching, mentoring (may I suggest Rapid's FastTrack program), training, or whatever other support you need in order to develop, improve and be more successful. Better still, be proactive and identify any courses or learning activities that will help you develop the skills you need to go to the next level.

6. Go next level: Finally, in your lead-up preparation, consider any promotion aspects for the year ahead. Where do you want to be at the end of the next twelve months? If you have ambitions to climb the corporate ladder, try to get hold of the position description for the next rung up. Review the selection criteria to see where you meet the criteria and identify any development areas you need to focus on.

7. Relax when stepping into the review: Nobody likes being judged, but two adults sitting down and talking about what you did right or wrong doesn't have to be as awkward as it sounds. Go into the review with an open mind. Maintain your mojo. Don't be nervous. Listen to everything your employer has to say, good or bad. Prepare yourself for your review by trying to relax and letting go of any defensiveness you're aware of. As with any interview, the best advice is to just be you.

8. To get your nose in front, take it on the chin: How you respond to negative criticism will reveal a lot about your workplace behaviour, maturity, personality and suitability for leadership. Take the time to listen and think, and then respond respectfully. Show that you're open to opportunities for growth and improvement. Don't get into arguments or try to pass blame. Accept that you can be wrong. Always try to be constructive with any negative feedback (hopefully you will have thought about it prior to the session).

9. Be fluent in body language: Much of our interactions with people involve non-verbal cues, a mixture of gestures, postures and expressions which some say can account for up to ninety percent of communication. The expression 'Your actions

speak louder than words' plays out in dramatic fashion in a performance review. Open up your posture to avoid the impression you're closed off. Don't roll your eyes in the face of negative criticism; keep a poker face. Maintain eye contact to build trust (but don't stare your manager down, keep it comfortable). Practise active listening. Nod along. Check-ins offer the chance for you to show your boss that you value them and their opinions.

10. Follow up after the review: Make sure you follow up on your performance review. Put your actions and due dates into your calendar or diary, with prompts along the way to work on these. Regardless of the feedback, always be thankful for it.

Performance reviews are an ideal time to discuss all the things you've achieved in the past year, but they're also a great opportunity to show how you're going to grow and bring even more value in the year ahead.

There is a difference between a bonus and a pay rise. A bonus is paid for the previous year's efforts where someone has gone above and beyond their requirements. It can also be paid if the business has done exceptionally well, and management has chosen to share some of the profits with employees. Bonuses should not be relied upon in any yearly salary calculations.

A pay rise is given when someone has shown they will deliver even more value in the year ahead—it is not a reward for good performance the previous year. When an employee demonstrates their development and the increased value they will bring to the company over the year ahead, they're offering fair evidence for a salary increase.

Knowing the commodity that your company sells and how they

make money is crucial to understanding your value proposition to the business. If you can demonstrate that over the year ahead you will deliver more billable hours, or charge yourself out at a higher rate, these are the areas that will make a salary-increase conversation more convincing.

Regardless of whether your organisation is a not-for-profit, government or private company, every business has customers and generates revenue through delivering value in some set way. If you show an intimate understanding of the core metrics around how your business operates, and how your role contributes to the larger business vision, you will be in a much better position to show how you add value, and know where to focus your efforts to increase your value to the organisation.

CONCLUSION

With the right routines, habits and mindset, I truly believe you can take your life and career further, faster. The high-performance tips outlined in this book will help you get more done in a day, either allowing you to earlier leave or get even *more* done. By striving to become a prominent person within your industry, and focusing on working your way up, you will put yourself in the right place to earn more, learn more, and add more value. Preparing for your performance reviews will help you maximise your salary by progressively pushing you towards your career goals.

I hope *Further Faster* will help you plan your own exciting journey, see all the marvellous sights along the way, and have an amazing adventure. The closing of this book is the opening of the next chapter in the rest of your life. I wish you all the best with living the life you desire, accompanied by the career of your dreams. Anything is possible with the right mindset, the right tools, and the right mentor.

I encourage you to focus on your four core pillars and assess how you're doing in each. Remember, there has to be balance to help you reach your highest goals.

Set intention for your life. Who do you want to be today, who do you want to be in ten years' time, and what do you want to be remembered for once you're gone?

Please get in touch and pass on your successes, your struggles and everything in between.

Strive forward with conviction, and may the future be yours!

MAKE MORE OUT OF YOUR LIFE AND CAREER IN LESS TIME

Want more insights? Make more of your life and career in less time with Rapid's FastTrack online mentoring program. It includes everything you need to know to live a happy, balanced and successful life. Discover the inside secrets and ideas you never learned in school or university, or at work.

What you get from Rapid Mentoring

Rapid Online Mentoring is here to help you develop resilience, motivation and performance, allowing you to take your life and career further, faster.

Rapid Mentoring is renowned for its extensive online learning platform. Members are issued exclusive access to our member portal, giving you a platform to guide your development with relevant and meaningful hints and tips. What it involves:

- Ten online learning modules, each containing worksheets, tools and further reading
- Ongoing learning via twice-weekly bite-sized emails to continue your development over the course of the 12-month subscription

- Ongoing interaction with Warren James, founder of the Rapid Online Mentoring program through emails, and monthly 15-minute one-to-one sessions

One-to-one time with Warren James, founder of Rapid Online Mentoring

- Ongoing email support with the Rapid Online Mentoring team over the course of the 12-month subscription
- One-to-one sessions via Skype or Zoom or phone: monthly 15-minute focus sessions

Online learning modules

- **Finance and Investing Module:** Educational material to help you get on top of your finances sooner. It covers what money is, along with the mistakes many people seem to make.
- **All-About-You Module:** The FastTrack to learning all about yourself—personality profiling, values assessments, building bucket lists, and delving deep into what makes you who you are.
- **Performance Review Module:** Take a deep dive into how to prepare for your next performance review.
- **Stress Management Module:** What is stress and how can you implement strategies to reduce it? It includes our Corporate Change Survivor Guide and many other practical tools to manage stress.

- **Purpose Module:** Find purpose, find direction, and find motivation.
- **Mental Strength Module:** Develop grit for when the going gets tough.
- **Personal-Development Module:** Get happy, and set personal goals for the future.
- **Future Planning Module:** Visualising the future and starting to build a roadmap to get there can be hugely motivational and even more rewarding.

In addition to the above, we also offer these bonuses:

- Weekly emails: Weekly bite-sized updates, gold nuggets and Q&A sessions from fellow members
- Monthly deep dive into our core areas (resilience, motivation or performance)
- Monthly book review sharing the insights from our favourite personal-development books
- Monthly member share where you hear what other members are up to and can learn from their experience; thrive in our community of like-minded members
- Monthly pearls of wisdom include interviews with industry heavy hitters to get their insights to help you go further, faster
- Private Facebook group to engage with other likeminded members

THE SCRIPT

If you're keen to join the Rapid Online Community, you can ask your employer to pay for it from your professional-development budget. Here is a cracking script to use in an email to your boss.

Dear [*boss's name*]

As you know, I am constantly looking for ways to improve my performance and to deliver greater value for [*name of organisation*]. There are many educational options available, and I know that we already have access to a number of those within [*name of organisation*]. In order to build on these programs, I have found an online mentoring program that will give me additional practical strategies that I can implement to accelerate my performance, enabling me to reach my full potential and drive better results for the company.

The program I have found is the Rapid Online Mentoring FastTrack program, which is delivered by Warren James, a guy whose main focus in life is helping the next generation take their lives and careers further, faster. I have read his book and have subscribed to his free weekly newsletter. I've found the content to be extremely relatable and I believe the content within the program could be of huge value to me and [*name of organisation*].

The program consists of a collection of life lessons everyone seems to learn the hard way. It covers things like stress management, career development, planning for the future, and high-performance techniques. It's delivered online over a full-year subscription, meaning I can log in when I want, where I want, and work through the online learning modules. They also send their members twice-weekly newsletters with deep dives, book reviews, industry heavy-hitter interviews, and Q&A sessions with the members.

Given my continual focus on improving my performance and leadership skills, and the additional value I know this will enable me to bring to [*name of organisation*], I would be grateful if you would consider [*name of organisation*] investing in this course for me.

Kind regards

[*your name*]

REFERENCES, RESOURCES AND FURTHER READING

Use this QR code to access the resources listed on these two pages.
Or visit https://rapidmentoring.com.au/bookresources/.

Websites

Ikigai (https://en.wikipedia.org/wiki/Ikigai)

Barefoot Investor (https://barefootinvestor.com/)

FIRE movement (https://en.wikipedia.org/wiki/FIRE_movement)

David R Hawkins' Map of Consciousness (https://www.pinterest.com.au/emotionalrelease/dr-david-hawkins/)

Jordan Harbinger's free 6 Minute Networking course (www.jordanharbinger.com/courses)

Online tests

16 Personalities (https://www.16personalities.com/)

Barrett Values Centre Assessment (https://www.valuescentre.com/tools-assessments/pva/)

Books

The Values Factor, Dr John Demartini
Purpose, Lisa Messenger
Key Person of Influence, Daniel Priestley
The Personal MBA, Josh Kaufman
The 10X Rule, Grant Cardone
Emotional Intelligence, Daniel Goleman
Atomic Habits, James Clear
Strengths Finder 2.0, Tom Rath
Deep Learning, Cal Newport
Stealing Fire, Steven Kotler and Jamie Wheal
Indistractable, Nir Eyal
High Performance Habits, Brendon Burchard
The Motivation Manifesto, Brendon Burchard

Rapid Mentoring resources

Rapid Mentoring homepage (https://rapidmentoring.com.au/)
Rapid Mentoring FastTrack program (https://rapidmentoring.com.au/fast-track/)
Rapid Mentoring blogs (https://rapidmentoring.com.au/blog/)
Rapid Debrief (https://rapidmentoring.com.au/bookresources/)
Rapid Sticky-Note Planner (https://rapidmentoring.com.au/bookresources/)
Rapid Priority Budget Tools (https://rapidmentoring.com.au/bookresources/)

www.ingramcontent.com/pod-product-compliance
Lightning Source LLC
Chambersburg PA
CBHW050311010526
44107CB00055B/2199